API

to

BEAR FRUIT

A Devotional Commentary on John 13-17

MICHAEL DENSMOOR

Appointed to Bear Fruit

By Michael Densmoor

Copyright © 2016 Michael Densmoor

ISBN-13: 978-0-9893362-1-5
1. Christianity. 2. Bible_Commentary.

DEDICATION

To my coworkers who are serving in difficult places. May
you always abound in the work of the Lord

Make Disciples

Now before the Feast of the Passover, when Jesus knew that his hour had come to depart out of this world to the Father...

– JOHN 13:1a

Read Matthew 28:16-20

If today was the last day of your life, what would you do with your final moments? Would you spend the day cooking and eating your favorite food? That doesn't seem too important since even after His resurrection Jesus still enjoyed a meal of grilled fish. Perhaps you would visit your favorite place one last time? That doesn't seem to be a good use of your time either since after His resurrection Jesus travelled to Galilee, a beautiful and refreshing place. We will have all of eternity to enjoy God's creation after He makes it new.

What task is so important that, with your final breath, you want to make sure it is completed and passed on to someone else? Maybe you think, "I want to share the gospel with my mother and father so that they will be saved, because this could be the last time that they will hear the Good News." Although that's a noble thing to do, it still is not the most important. Your final activities should reflect the most important task of your life. Jesus' example on the final night before His crucifixion highlights what that is for us as believers. Surprisingly, He doesn't perform one final, incredible miracle so that the maximum number of people will witness it and repent. And He doesn't hold a revival meeting in the courtyard of the Temple so that many will hear from the Lamb of God for the last time.

So what did Jesus do? In His final moments, He does a single thing. He gathered His disciples and taught them again about who Christ is and how they were to carry out His mission. If you understand that the purpose of discipleship is to prepare people to go and make disciples, then when the time comes and you are no longer here, your ministry will continue on through the lives of your disciples. If your ministry is only done by yourself, others will hear the gospel and be saved—and that could be where it ends. You will meet your disciples in heaven, but your reunion will be attended by only a few people. However, if you raise up other disciples, once you are gone, they will continue to reach many more people and you will be part of a greater rejoicing in heaven as the multitude of believers gather together. In other words, you will have multiplied your efforts in a far greater way for the Kingdom of God.

So many have yet to grasp the exciting potential that is within every disciple. Once we see it, it makes training disciples who make disciples so much more important than trying to achieve only results through our personal ministry. A good servant of God is one who reaches *many* souls. Proclaiming the gospel to those who have never heard it before is an important ministry, *but the greatest servant of God is one who equips others to go and reach their own people with the gospel.* Ministry that relies solely on us will end once we leave this earth. If we invest ourselves in preparing others to go and make disciples, then our ministry will have a much greater impact.

On Jesus' last night, what did He impart to His disciples that was so important that He neglected all other ministry opportunities and, instead, spent these final hours with only a few? That is the context of John 13-17. These chapters reveal Jesus' activities to us on this final night—the final hours of His ministry—and His final teachings to those who would continue in His work. Are you investing your life in making disciples who will make disciples?

Serving Out of Love

...having loved his own who were in the world, he loved them to the end.

– JOHN 13:1b

Read I Timothy 1:12-20

People serve the Lord out of many different motives. Some serve out of *guilt*. They may equate not sharing the gospel with not being good Christians. Personally, I never liked being asked at church at the end of the year: "How many people have you won to the Lord this past year?" This is the wrong question. I am not able to convince anyone to follow Jesus. The appropriate question is: "How many people have you shared the gospel with?" God is the one who uses our gospel presentations to penetrate hard hearts and draw people to Himself. And some places are naturally more receptive to the gospel than others. Some of us serve among "nominal" Christians who have had the gospel for generations. In such places, it's not surprising to see a great response when the gospel is proclaimed.

But others of us minister among "resistive" people. The seeds of the gospel have been faithfully sown, but few of those seeds have grown into faith. When asked how many people have been won to the Lord, you can feel a sense of guilt, because even though you have faithfully served the Lord, there's been little response. Those feelings of guilt, if not careful, can be soothed by answering the question untruthfully so that we won't feel judged by others. The key is to be faithful to what the Lord has entrusted to us. We need to fulfill the responsibility God has given to us without comparing ourselves to others. Those working among "resistive" people can often struggle with guilt, because they feel that the fruit of their labor doesn't justify the expense of keeping them in that ministry assignment. But, God desires us to faithfully do the work that He has assigned to us. He is responsible for the results, so we just need to be faithful. We need to focus on our portion of kingdom work as a good steward and not worry about the rest!

Although some of us fall into the trap of ministering out of guilt, others may do it to *show off*. When I first arrived in my place of ministry, I had a strong desire for people to recognize that I was a success. I wanted them to see all that *I* did. I built relationships with important people with the hope that my name would become known to many. My motivation was to serve in a manner that was seen by others. I knew this was sin. At the root of this sin was my own insecurity in Christ. I wasn't satisfied with myself and with God's work in my life, so I tried to replace His work with mine. We also see this happening in the Apostle Peter's life. He was always trying to make something happen on his own, because He wasn't patient in waiting for God to act.

Jesus; however, ministers with a completely different motivation. Everything He does is done out of *love*. So great is the love of Christ that He gave Himself as a ransom for many. He was willing to be humiliated and considered unimportant so that we could be saved. He let people use Him to obtain blessings, while these same people were rejecting the truth about Him. Why was Jesus willing to suffer all these things for us? Because of love. He knew that the world was polluted by sin. Being secure in His position, He was able to serve out of the pure motive of love. If we are unsure that we have a throne waiting for us in heaven, we will work to obtain a throne here on earth. *The more we are certain that God loves us unconditionally, the more we will serve out of a pure heart motive.*

Christ didn't only give us a new command to love one another; He came near to us and demonstrated that love in practical and sacrificial ways. Jesus didn't give orders to the world from far way, rather He took part in our daily lives. Likewise, we serve others according to the example of Christ. We must become part of their lives—and minister out of a pure motive of love. What is your motive for serving?

Pursuing the Father's Interests

During supper, when the devil had already put it into the heart of Judas Iscariot, Simon's son, to betray him, Jesus, knowing that the Father had given all things into his hands, and that he had come from God and was going back to God...

– JOHN 13:2-3

Read II Corinthians 12:1-10

The biggest enemy to your ministry is your pride. You cannot serve the Lord if you are not humble. Your pride will keep you from being formed into the image of Christ, because you won't listen to advice from others or correction from God's Word. The proud heart doesn't want to be told what to do but, instead, wants to be the one telling everyone else what to do. Proud people think they know better than everyone else. Sadly, your God-given strengths for service often become an obstacle to growing in spiritual maturity.

Without humility, no one can be a disciple. I believe this is key. I am a member of The Reformed Evangelical Church of Indonesia. The word "reformed" reminds us that God's Word defines our faith. The word "evangelical" refers to the commitment to proclaim the gospel. These two words are put together to show that we need to have not just the right content of our faith, but also the right passion. Yet I have always felt that there was a word missing in the denomination's name. Not only is it important to focus on content and passion, but there must also be an emphasis on character. In my opinion, the name should be: The Reformed Evangelical Church of Humble Servants.

Many intelligent people understand the Bible but in their hearts, they still idolize themselves. A person can have great enthusiasm for the Lord, but without humility they can destroy the faith of many. That's why we can't be of service to God's kingdom without humility. I know of many young people who leave their villages to attend Bible college. But something happens once they receive their diploma: they become boastful. They proudly announce, "Now I am a servant of God." A servant of *who*? They haven't done anything except receive a piece of paper and already they are making demands or refusing ministry assignments, because the assignments are not to their liking. Some demand that a church provides them with certain benefits. After all, they surmise, they deserve it. It's better not to receive a diploma if it leads to pride and instead to be used by God in the place He wants you than to serve Him with fleshy, sinful motives.

We can start out well, but fail along the way. We have to complete the course that God wants us to run. The Apostle Paul spoke about running the race that God had set out before him. Paul had amazing spiritual experiences. He had met Jesus personally on the Road to Damascus and received his revelation directly from Jesus (Gal. 1:12-17). Throughout his ministry, Paul did miraculous works like raising the dead. He brought the gospel to lands and peoples who had never heard about Christ. To top it all off, Paul experienced being caught up to the third heaven and witnessed incredible things (II Cor. 12:2-4). Yet, despite all the amazing spiritual experiences, Paul was afraid that he would disqualify himself from receiving the reward of his service. Paul knew the danger of pride that might prevent him from reaching the finish line.

Your humility will determine how God uses you in the future. Nearly every problem that disqualifies us for service has its roots in pride. Judas disqualified himself because of pride. He didn't want to submit to the Father's plan. And because the Father would not follow Judas' plan, Judas betrayed Jesus. But Jesus is humble. He boldly submitted to the Father's plan even though He knew that the Father had given all things to Jesus. Humility led Jesus to put aside His own interests so that the will of the Father would be accomplished. We too must do likewise. Every day we must live humbly before God so that His plans will be manifested in us. Will you pursue the Father's interests?

Wash Some Feet

[Jesus] rose from supper. He laid aside his outer garments, and taking a towel, tied it around his waist. Then he poured water into a basin and began to wash the disciples' feet and to wipe them with the towel that was wrapped around him.

– JOHN 13:4-5

Read Matthew 20:20-28

Jesus always strived to glorify the Father's name rather than His own earthly reputation. Because Jesus knew that the Father had prepared a throne for Him in heaven, He didn't need to defend His earthly rights. For instance, Jesus ate with tax collectors. By eating in the house of those viewed as outright sinners by the religious leaders, Jesus was ruining His reputation. *Jesus' concern was not for His name, but that the Father would be glorified as sinners repented.* Even in front of His own disciples, Jesus humbled Himself and washed their feet. He didn't care how humiliating it was because, the following day, Jesus would suffer even greater humiliation as He hung on the cross. When Jesus washed His disciples' feet, Jesus was only humiliated in front of 12 people, His disciples. But the next day, not only would His robe be removed, He would have no garment at all to cover Himself with. He would not kneel only before His disciples, but would be nailed to a cross in front of the entire world. Washing His disciples' feet was not so humiliating compared to what was soon to come in His crucifixion.

Notice the difference between Christ and ourselves. Christ's first response is always humility. For us, it's often pride. We don't want our names to be viewed poorly. In fact, we are often striving to make our names greater. Christ's example of washing His disciples' feet invites us to evaluate our own hearts. To what extent are you willing to be humbled for the glory of God's name? A mature disciple is one who doesn't need to be honored by the world. Their desire is to only honor God. *Those used by God are committed to putting God's name above all else.* After nearly 400 years without a prophet in Israel, John the Baptist appeared on the scene. Certainly, the Jews gave him great deference and honor. Instead of being honored by men, however, John the Baptist chose to live in the wilderness and die alone in prison. Yet John the Baptist was the greatest man because he knew that he must decrease in importance so that all the focus would be put on Christ (John 3:30).

As Jesus and His disciples travelled to Jerusalem to celebrate the Passover, the disciples were fighting among themselves. Jesus had just told them that He would be put to death in Jerusalem. Instead of preparing their hearts for what was about to happen, the disciples were arguing over who would be the greatest in the kingdom. Jesus rebuked them saying that if they wanted to be the greatest they had to become a servant, and if they wanted to be exalted they needed to live in humility. A few days later, Jesus entered Jerusalem as the crowd shouted, "Hosanna, Hosanna!" As the disciples witnessed this scene, perhaps they were thinking that this was the moment when Jesus would take control of the land, and they would rule with Him. What an amazing accomplishment for a bunch of village men. Unfortunately, the disciples were caught up in the earthly accolades instead of identifying with the teachings of Jesus.

Jesus' teaching turns the world's view upside down. He says, "To be great you must become a servant." Don't let the temptations of this world lead you astray and into disobedience. Many who serve the Lord focus on what's in it for them. Satan is always trying to buy your calling. He even tried it with Jesus by offering Him all the kingdoms of the world if Jesus would only worship him. If the disciples had thought, "I want to glorify God's name and not my own," then they would have been willing to wash each other's' feet. Because His disciples weren't willing, Jesus humbled Himself and washed their feet. Whose feet do you need to wash?

Humble Yourself

He came to Simon Peter, who said to him, "Lord, do you wash my feet?" Jesus answered him, "What I am doing you do not understand now, but afterward you will understand." Peter said to him, "You shall never wash my feet."

— JOHN 13:6-8a

Read James 4:1-10

The humble Jesus washed the feet of all His disciples. The Lord, the Great Teacher, washed their feet one by one until He reached Peter. It's not hard to imagine how uncomfortable Peter must have felt as Jesus knelt before him. Like Peter, we are also uncomfortable when we find ourselves in situations that we know are not as they should be. We may feel bad, but how willing are we to correct the situation by doing the right thing? For example, we might find ourselves in a situation where someone wants to buy something for us so we are obligated to them. We pretend as though we don't want it saying, "Please don't. You don't need to buy that for me." But we end up accepting it anyway, even though we know we will be indebted to them. Our hearts are uneasy with what is happening, but we don't have the courage to do the right thing. Peter's heart was uncomfortable, so he tried to reject Jesus' service saying, "Do you wash my feet?" His feet were dirty and needed to be washed.

When Jesus knelt before Peter, immediately Peter showed His true colors. With great pride Peter said to Jesus, "You shall never wash my feet." Jesus' humility is contrasted with Peter's pride. Once again, Peter was telling Jesus what to do. How prideful! "You shall never wash my feet," he told Jesus. But, Jesus wanted to do it, and Peter was forbidding him. Peter always seemed to be telling Jesus how to act. On another occasion, Jesus said, "We are going to Jerusalem, and there I will be arrested, mocked and killed." After Jesus said this, Peter took Him aside and rebuked Him saying that Jesus should not say these things (Matt. 16:21-22). Peter thought that if Jesus kept talking about dying, then His disciples would become nervous. He believed that it was better for Jesus to conquer Jerusalem as king instead of dying as a martyr.

Be careful that, in your pride, you don't order God around. Satan wanted to rule rather than be ruled. He wanted to be worshipped rather than give worship to God. This was Satan's sin. It was Adam and Eve's sin. It was also Peter's sin. And it is ours as well. True disciples want to be humble in heart like the Lord. They don't seek high positions for themselves, but are content in a lowly state. They don't grow accustomed to being served by others, but are prepared to serve. As much as possible, I try to do things for myself so that others can use their time to spread the gospel, instead of taking care of me. On one occasion, I visited North Africa where they only speak French or Arabic. I only speak English and Indonesian. The pastor was prepared to drive 10 hours round-trip to pick me up at the airport. If I let him do that, he would have spent his entire day just being my driver. Instead, I told him I could get there myself. I made my way to the bus station and got to his town on my own.

Striving to do things for yourself so that you can respect other people's time and ministry is a characteristic of humility. No one is the boss. All believers are servants. Pick up your towel! Follow the example of our Lord. Have you been ordering God around or submitting to Him?

Confess Your Sins

Jesus answered him, "If I do not wash you, you have no share with me." Simon Peter said to him, "Lord, not my feet only but also my hands and my head!" Jesus said to him, "The one who has bathed does not need to wash, except for his feet, but is completely clean."

– JOHN 13:8b-10a

Read James 1:19-25

Even though Peter had been struggling with pride, he was finally learning to listen to the Lord's words. This time, He didn't correct what Jesus said about the meaning of the washing. Instead, he finally got it and embraced Jesus' ministry with great enthusiasm. Yet, the result was the same. Peter gave orders to Christ. "Lord, not my feet only but also my hands and my head!" What a sight that must have been. Imagine Peter stripping down to his underwear during the meal, with all the other disciples watching him take a bath. After hearing Jesus say that He must wash their feet, Peter immediately wanted to supersede the Lord's command. His devotion to God was so great that he was always trying to do more than what was desired. Peter once again fell into the same problem. First, he rejected to be served by Jesus. Now, he was telling Jesus how to serve Him. Peter continued to position himself higher than Jesus.

No one can tell God what to do, so don't deceive yourself. As a leader, it's easy to think that because you have authority to tell others what to do, you can also do the same with God. Once you start down that path, it won't be long before you believe that God's job is to serve *your* needs instead of the other way around. *Humility means that you desire to be made into God's image so that His name is made holy and is respected.*

Jesus corrected Peter by saying, "The one who has bathed does not need to wash, except for his feet, but is completely clean." Here, Jesus revealed the secret of

11

washing. Once you have been made clean by the blood of Jesus, you don't need to receive Jesus a second time. Your sins have been forgiven for all time. And, you don't need to be baptized more than once. (Baptism is the sign of repentance: a sign that you have been made clean by the blood of Christ.) Bathing and washing are different. Those who have been bathed are clean. But, throughout the day, dirt gathers on parts of our bodies and needs to be washed off. In the same way, we who have been made clean through repentance still commit sins. We desire to live holy lives in accordance with God's plan, but we are not fully able to. That's where humility comes in. When we sin, we need to *humbly* come before God and confess our sins.

Some of us refuse to accept responsibility for our sin. Instead, we live in denial or blame it on someone else. On one occasion, a man came to us wanting to join our ministry. He had been accused of having an inappropriate relationship with a woman and was subsequently dismissed. In his interview, the man explained how the whole thing was a misunderstanding and that he was falsely accused. His explanation seemed reasonable so he joined our ministry on a probationary status. It wasn't even three months before he was involved in another inappropriate relationship. It's troubling how people can so easily deny their sins instead of humbling themselves and confessing their sins. None of us can play with God. In the same way that Adam and Eve tried to cover their nakedness with leaves, so too we try to cover our nakedness before God with flimsy excuses. These excuses merely point out our problem with pride.

You need to be responsible for your own actions. Instead of defending yourself and blaming God or others, a humble disciple will confess their sin saying, "Lord, I have sinned today. Wash me clean, for my feet are dirty with sin." What sins do you need to confess today?

Repent

"And you are clean, but not every one of you." For he knew who was to betray him; that was why he said, "Not all of you are clean."

– JOHN 13:10b-11

Read Matthew 7:15-23

As mentioned in John 13:1, the Son of God knew that the time had arrived to fulfill the Father's plan of salvation. Even though Jesus knew that Judas was going to betray Him, Jesus still washed Judas' feet. Instead of inflicting harm on Judas, Jesus knelt before Judas and washed the dirt from his feet. In these final moments before His arrest, Jesus was still giving Judas an opportunity to repent. Judas witnessed the miracles performed by Jesus. Judas had heard the teachings of Jesus that left the crowds amazed. He was even sent out by Jesus to proclaim the Good News of God's Kingdom. Few were as privileged as Judas to experience such blessings. However, none of it ever penetrated Judas' heart. He was not clean.

Many people serve and work diligently for God, yet they have never repented by asking Christ into their heart. We are too quick to see the external activities and assume that these activities represent the internal reality of their hearts. Good works and religious service don't make someone pleasing to God. Repentance is the ministry of the Holy Spirit that convicts us of our sin and brings us to Christ. Our good works and ministry are our response to the grace of God that has saved us. It is sad that many believe that the Lord is pleased with them because of their service in His name. Everyone needs to be cleansed by the Holy Spirit so that they are acceptable to God.

It's easy for people to exploit religion and even Christ to further their personal ambitions. They serve because it will give them status, power, or wealth. From their mouths are heard beautiful religious platitudes, yet they are controlled by Satan. Their hearts are full of sinful passions

13

like jealousy, anger, and lust. They prioritize riches over Christ. Judas was one such person. Outwardly, he appeared to be a true disciple, yet it was all a deception. When he said that money should not be wasted, but instead be used to help the poor, Judas was at that time stealing money from Jesus' ministry (John 12:4-6).

The world judges by looking at externals, but God looks at the internal reality. God judges the heart. From the externals, it seemed like Peter and not Judas was the problem disciple. Peter was always putting his foot in his mouth, and his actions showed a lack of faith. Judas, on the other hand, appeared to be filled with compassion for the poor and was so responsible that Jesus appointed him the treasurer of His ministry. But Peter was the one accepted by the Lord. Judas was rejected. Why? Because Peter was clean and Judas wasn't. *It's better to serve with people who submit to God even though they often make mistakes than serve with those who appear to do great ministry, but are under the control of Satan.* Do not compromise on this. Peter was arrogant, but Judas was a hypocrite. Arrogant people can learn humility through Jesus' work in their lives, but hypocrites never have a place in God's work or kingdom.

Christ repeatedly gave opportunities to Judas to repent. However, Judas refused them all. His heart should have been filled with grief and repentance when Jesus washed his feet, but that didn't happen. Don't be like Judas who betrayed Christ because God's plans were not the same as his plans. Submit to God's will for your life. His plans will not disappoint you. Have you truly repented?

God Bestows Honor on The Humble

When he had washed their feet and put on his outer garments and resumed his place, he said to them, "Do you understand what I have done to you?"

– JOHN 13:10b-12

Read Mark 8:31-38

John 13 begins with Jesus removing his garment and putting on the wardrobe of a servant. After He finished being misunderstood while He washed the disciples' feet, as well as being told what to do by those who did not want to listen, Jesus once again put on His outer garment. This foot-washing event was a living parable of how Jesus was fulfilling the Father's plan of salvation. Jesus left His throne in heaven, was born in a stable, was despised by the religious leaders, exploited by the crowds, betrayed by a close friend, and then ridiculed and brutally murdered. After all of this, Jesus rose again and ascended into heaven where He once again was adorned with the glory that was His from the beginning. When Jesus took off His garment, humbled Himself as a servant, and then put back on His garment, He was illustrating for His disciples the reality of His incarnation and His coming ascension.

Becoming like Christ means that we imitate Jesus' example to deny ourselves in order to fulfill the Father's redemptive plan. Paul writes in Philippians 3:10 that he desires to become, "like him in his death." When we contemplate becoming like Christ, we usually only think about the moral attributes of Christ's character. We want to be more loving, live more holy lives, and so on. But Paul tells us that becoming like Christ also includes becoming like Him in His death. Many Christians only want the benefits of a relationship with God. Rarely does one pray that God would cause them to die to themselves so that they would grow in Christ-likeness. *Disciples surrender themselves to*

God. In His time, God will exchange our humility on earth with His honor in heaven.

It is a real shame that the disciples did not understand this. As they headed to Jerusalem, Jesus spoke about self-denial. His disciples, instead, jostled for position and power. This world places a premium on status and power. We feel it is so burdensome to deny ourselves and serve in situations where we are misunderstood and humiliated. Our eyes take in the world's values of status and position, creating a divided heart. We want to follow Christ, but we also want the comforts of this world. Satan tempts us with the lie that you can have both Christ and this world. The result is that we go along with the spirit of this age instead of becoming disciples that *change* this age. It's hard for us to accept that God's plan is fulfilled through the way of the cross.

"Do you understand what I have done to you?" What an important question. The disciples had been particularly slow to understand God's plan. When Jesus taught about the Kingdom of God using parables, the disciples couldn't understand the message. Even after the resurrection, the disciples still didn't understand. They only understood the Father's plan after the Spirit was given to them. The Spirit is the one who reveals the secrets of God. Every disciple has been given the Spirit so that they will understand the plan of God that is announced throughout the Scripture.

Ask the Holy Spirit to give you understanding about the great work of Christ. Only through understanding and meditating on Christ's sacrifice will we find victory over the temptations of Satan and this world. God is calling us to a lifestyle that is vastly different from the ways of this world. He wants us to make decisions based on the example of Christ and not on worldly priorities. Becoming a mature disciple means that we carry our cross through denying ourselves daily. It is this surrendering that is essential for discipleship. Christ was willing to surrender Himself and pay the price. Are you willing to pay the price required to fulfill God's plan for your life?

The Value System of Heaven

*You call me Teacher and Lord, and you are right, for so I am. If I
then, your Lord and Teacher, have washed your feet, you also ought
to wash one another's feet.*

– JOHN 13:13-14

Read Philippians 2:1-5

I find it interesting how, in Indonesia, when two
people meet for the first time they introduce themselves in
such a way to determine which of them has the higher
status. This is important so that the person with the lower
status can give deference to the person of higher status. The
world links status with honor. In the world's system, the one
who washes the feet is in the lower position. The one whose
feet is washed is the greater person. Following the world's
logic, we could conclude that if Jesus who washes the feet
is Lord and Teacher, then the disciples are greater than God.
Jesus turned the world's system of power upside down.
*When the world's system and values meet the Lord, the world's system
immediately collapses.*

I am often surprised by the words of Jesus. This is one
of those surprising statements. After Jesus finished washing
their feet, Jesus should have told them: "If I then, your Lord
and Teacher, have washed your feet, you also ought to wash
My feet." In room where they gathered, it should have been
a madhouse with all 12 disciples fighting over the privilege
of washing Jesus' feet. But that's not what Jesus told them
to do. He never asked them to wash His feet. Instead, He
told them to wash each other's feet.

Think about how difficult that would be. The higher
our opinion is of ourselves and the more we feel needed by
our ministry, the greater the danger we face of becoming
prideful. Our culture says that the lesser serves the greater.
But in Jesus' ministry, the greatest is the least. It is the one
that serves with humility that is awarded the greatest honor.

Jesus teaches us that it is not the lesser that serves the greater. Interestingly, He also doesn't teach that the greater serves the lesser. He says that we are all servants who serve one another. Jesus' teachings are superior to all the philosophies of the world and harder to implement by sinners like us.

Jesus asks the disciples to do the better thing. In other words, don't be satisfied with a level 7 humility. Pursue level 10 humility. You can never be humble enough. Compared to 20 years ago, I am much humbler. God has been at work in me through the various ministry experiences I have had. My fellowship with other believers has also helped me to grow in humility. But if I am satisfied with my current level of humility, I am in danger of becoming prideful again. I may be humble enough to wash Jesus' feet. I may even be humble enough to wash the feet of those who return the favor. *But am I willing to serve those who do not return my service with similar actions, but betray me instead?* Serving one another is not too lowly a task. It's so much more humbling to serve the betrayers among us just like Jesus did.

It's also important to remember why Jesus' feet did not need washing. Jesus instructed the disciples that foot washing was a symbol of being made clean through the confession of sins, so that we will have restored fellowship with God. Each of us sin and need cleansing through confession. Jesus is the only one without sin. Yet, Christ identified Himself with our sins through His baptism so that He, as the Lamb of God, would take away the sins of the world. Jesus didn't need cleansing because He was sinless.

All of the disciples' feet were clean. And, even Judas ate the meal with clean feet. Jesus' feet were dirty with the dust from the road, but soon it would not only be dust that made His feet dirty but the blood and sweat that would flow down His body as He bore our sin on the cross. "He who knew no sins was made sin for us so that we might have eternal life" (II Cor. 5:21). To what extent does the world's system influence your heart and mind?

Joy and Humility

For I have given you an example, that you also should do just as I have done to you. Truly, truly, I say to you, a servant is not greater than his master, nor is a messenger greater than the one who sent him. If you know these things, blessed are you if you do them.

– JOHN 13:15-17

Read Matthew 5:1-12

One thing that is particularly wonderful in Indonesia is the splendid service provided by those in the hospitality business. For example, when you attend a wedding reception you are greeted by the friendliest people. These greeters make sure that you are well cared for. To be honest, it's a joy to be served by people like this. It makes me feel special. But what is more impressive is the attitude of those who are serving. The greeters' faces radiate with smiles showing how much joy they derive from assisting you. They reflect how blessed they are through their service to you.

Everyone wants to be filled with joy. Since people's relationship with God has been ruined by sin, they often try to medicate their unhappiness with riches, popularity, and entertainment. But it's not until after we believe in Christ that we receive the abundant life Christ promised, and enjoy all the blessings of heaven. In the Sermon on the Mount, Jesus repeatedly told His listeners that those who abide in Him will be blessed. In the Upper Room, Jesus again affirms this truth. Obeying the commands of Jesus will bring blessing.

A humble life is also a blessed life. From the world's view these two things seem contradictory. It's human nature to rule rather than be ruled. In our flesh, we fight with wanting to serve others rather than being served ourselves. This is an area where Satan continually tempts us to live according to our flesh instead by the Spirit. But, we must choose daily who we will serve. We can choose to be filled with pride like Peter was and order Christ around, or we can follow the example of the humble Christ. *We can fight against our flesh with the weapon of repentance by praying humbly, "Lord, I am a sinner. Help me to serve You and others. Forgive my proud heart."* When we are willing to become the least, God will flood our hearts with His joy and blessedness.

It should be our goal to pursue joy in serving others. This is the fruit of humility. Our flesh; however, works to ruin this fruit. Christ always tells us the truth even if we don't like to hear it. He says that His servants are not greater than Himself—our Master. If Christ was ridiculed, spit on, swore at, then we should expect similar treatment. We are not greater than Christ. Yet for many of us, we desire to follow Christ, but are unwilling to pay the high price of discipleship. We want the blessings without the cross.

It can be tough to be humiliated and disrespected by your ministry partners. It can make us feel defeated and discouraged. But none of us are superman. I, too, am weak and find it challenging to continually serve in situations like this. These situations can rob us of our joy, if we let them. Without joy, it's easy to fall back into living according to the flesh. Joy is like engine oil. Even when high temperatures strain the engine, the oil keeps everything functioning smoothly. The joy of a humble heart is possible, because we are doing God's will rather than following our own foolishness or fleshly desires. After the disciples were arrested, imprisoned, and beaten, they were released and went home filled with joy because they were counted worthy to suffer for the name of Jesus (Acts 5:41). This is the blessing that Jesus promised in Matthew 5:11-12. There is a heavenly blessing in store for those who are persecuted, because of Christ's name—joy is one of those blessings. Is your pride robbing you of joy?

Your Future Is in God's Hands

I am not speaking of all of you; I know whom I have chosen. But the Scripture will be fulfilled, 'He who ate my bread has lifted his heel against me.' I am telling you this now, before it takes place, that when it does take place you may believe that I am he.

– JOHN 13:18-19

Read Mark 14:10-21

We can be confident that those who deny themselves and are humble in heart will not be disappointed by Christ. When we are courageous enough to obey Christ and follow Him, we will be filled with confidence that our future is indeed secure in Christ. He invites us to go against our flesh and the world's norms. *Self-denial and serving others means placing your future in the hands of God.*

As believers, our confidence is founded in the omniscience of Christ who was never surprised by any situation that occurred. When Jesus wanted to eat the Passover meal in Jerusalem with His disciples, He gave them instructions, saying: "Go into the city, and a man carrying a jar of water will meet you" (Mark 14:13). Jesus knew exactly who would be passing by, when, and carrying what. Everything was known by Jesus. He also knew that He was going to be betrayed by Judas and would be arrested that very night in Gethsemane. Because of His knowledge of what was to come, it would have been easy for Jesus to avoid Gethsemane and escape the trap that was set for Him. But He didn't.

Once they had Jesus in their custody, the Jewish leaders treated Jesus with cruelty and humiliation. Then after the Sanhedrin had condemned the Son from Heaven for blaspheming God, several people covered Jesus' head and "spit in his face and struck him. And some slapped him, saying, 'Prophesy to us, you Christ! Who is it that struck you?'" (Matt. 26:67-68). Don't be mistaken. If Jesus knew the position of a person carrying a water jug through a busy city, He certainly knew who hit Him. Nonetheless, Jesus let them treat Him like this because He knew that everything that was happening was part of God's plan to pay our debt of sin.

Yes, it was easy for doubts to arise about whether Jesus really was the Son of God. As long as Jesus was showing His power through the working of miracles, people believed that He was the Christ. But now that He seemed powerless to even defend Himself, people were reconsidering their beliefs about Christ. Perhaps some thought that He was a fraud or that God had left Him. We should not doubt Christ even in the darkest of times. Jesus knew what was to come, so He prepared His disciples beforehand by telling them all that would happen. He knew precisely who, how, and when He would be handed over to the Jews. After all, it had been prophesied more than 1,000 years earlier in Psalm 41:9. The Father's plan to redeem us from our sins through the Son's death on the cross was set in motion from the beginning and not suddenly thought up by the Father.

Jesus said that He was telling them all these things so that they would know that He is God. When the situation appeared bleak, Jesus testified about Himself. Even His betrayal by a close friend could not derail the Father's plan. Although there seemed to be no hope, it's exactly at that moment that Christ shown His light in the darkness. "I am he." All the attacks of the devil cannot destroy Christ's testimony about Himself. Instead, it was through the cross that once and for all He defeated Satan. Are you confidently placing your future in God's hands?

Seeking the Approval Of God

Truly, truly, I say to you, whoever receives the one I send receives me, and whoever receives me receives the one who sent me.

– JOHN 13:20

Read Matthew 10:5-33

Being received is the opposite of being rejected. Followers of Jesus can expect one of these two reactions from the world. Jesus knew firsthand about rejection. He came to the Jews to offer them eternal life, but the religious leaders rejected Him. Jesus was even rejected by one of His closest companions, Judas. Because of this reality, Jesus prepares His disciples to face rejection from the world. In the same way that Jesus was rejected, so too will His disciples be rejected because "a disciple is not above his teacher, nor a servant above his master" (Matt. 10:24). *Being humble and denying ourselves means being willing to be rejected.* Humanly speaking nobody wants to be rejected. We want to be liked by others. And as long as we go with the flow of this world, we will be embraced by it. But if we follow Christ, the world will reject us. Jesus is the dividing line. No one can stay neutral when confronted by the reality that they are sinners. You either accept the message of salvation brought by Christ or you reject it and continue in your sin.

We are sent into this world, however, not to adapt to the ways of this world but to live for God and testify about Christ. Our commission is not from an organization or other people. We are sent by Christ Himself. That is why we must obey Christ's command to proclaim the gospel. There is no other gospel that we can offer the world other than "Jesus Christ is Lord, to the glory of God the Father" (Phil. 2:11) who "gave himself as a ransom for all" (I Tim. 2:6). The world can reject the Good News, but there is no other news to share with them. Christ has tasked us with spreading this message everywhere that He sends us to.

When we are rejected we must remember that it is not

us that people are rejecting, but Him who sent us. They reject us in the name of Christ, but in reality, it is Christ that they are rejecting. Our goal is not to be popular with many followers. Christ did not send us to gather a large group. Our job is simply to go to those who have been prepared by God to hear and respond to His gospel. Those who receive this gospel are not only receiving us, but are receiving the Lord who sent us. As a result, eternal life is given and they are now in Christ. Because of the gospel which has saved them, they no longer have to work futilely to pay their debt of sin. It is Christ who has redeemed them.

There is no ministry more glorious than to be sent by Jesus to take the gospel to others. Our enthusiasm for this task should never wane no matter what cost must be paid. Jesus paid the greatest price to fulfill the Father's plan of salvation. He denied Himself and died on the cross. We must do the same by serving with humility and, through self-denial, bearing the same scorn and rejection because of our proclamation of the Good News. Fortunately, we know that not everyone will reject us. Some will receive us, meaning they will receive Jesus, and receiving Jesus means receiving the Father and His plan of salvation. Our witness is powerful. It is not because of who *we* are, but because we bring Christ. The gospel is the power to save regardless of who proclaims it. So we model our witness on the work of Christ. We give ourselves through self-sacrifice so that others will hear the gospel. Certainly, we will experience periods of difficulty, but the Lord will be with us. God will lead us to those whom He has prepared to receive Christ. Are you seeking the approval of others or of God?

God's Plan Is Costly

After saying these things, Jesus was troubled in his spirit, and testified, "Truly, truly, I say to you, one of you will betray me." The disciples looked at one another, uncertain of whom he spoke.

– JOHN 13:21-22

Read Mark 14:1-9

The disciples gathered with Jesus to celebrate an important event in the life of the Jews. The Passover celebration was a time of rejoicing as they remembered how the Lord freed the Jews from their slavery in Egypt. God never forgot His people. In the depths of their oppression in Egypt, the Jews called out to God. And God rescued them. He did what was considered impossible by freeing more than two million people from Egypt. Certainly, the Jews celebrated this day with great rejoicing.

But in the midst of this joyful celebration, Jesus was troubled in His spirit. Jesus experienced a similar feeling when He stood at the grave of Lazarus. The reality of death troubled Jesus. God's plan was that we would live and not die. But sin brought death upon us. Because of the reality of death, God promised to redeem us from our sin just as He redeemed the Jews from their slavery in Egypt on the Passover. *Jesus was troubled in spirit because soon He would fulfill that which was symbolized by the Passover. He would set us free from our slavery to Satan and sin.* The price of our redemption would be paid by Jesus Himself. Even though Jesus was God, He was also fully man. In His humanity, Jesus understood what was about to transpire and His heart was deeply moved.

All the events of that night and the following day didn't happen because of the betrayal of Judas, the hatred of the Jewish leaders, or the wickedness of the Roman occupiers. Everything occurred according to *God's* plan. Judas' betrayal did not catch Jesus by surprise. Jesus reminded Judas that heaven was orchestrating the events that night. Not even someone as evil as Judas could oppose God's plans. When we face difficulties and are attacked by Satan and the world, we need to take comfort in knowing that God is ruling in heaven. Our assailants cannot overcome God's plan. The Lord is permitting them to act against us in order to fulfill His perfect will.

The disciples were confused by Jesus' announcement. How is it possible that one of His disciples could do such a thing? Those of us in ministry know that our co-workers often disappoint us. Some are always trying to show off, but only end up putting their foot in their mouths just as Peter did on so many occasions. Others are like Judas who smile on the outside, while stabbing us in the back. When we focus on our co-workers' impure motives and sinful actions, we can easily grow weary and want to give up the work. Opposition from the outside causes us to pull together in unity and persevere in prayer to defeat the challenges we face. But problems that come from within are more difficult to face. Throughout our time of ministry together, we have built a camaraderie based on our mutual experiences. Times of opposition have taught us to trust our co-workers. When our trusted co-workers turn on us and betray us, we are filled with crushing disappointment. We expect the world to reject us, but how is it possible that our co-workers could be so cruel to us, we ask.

After hearing Jesus' announcement, the disciples immediately wondered who it was that Jesus was referring to. They could not figure out who Jesus meant. *Sadly, Jesus' followers were unable to differentiate between a true disciple and a false disciple.* Throughout their ministry together, the disciples often argued among themselves. In their minds, every one of the other disciples was a possible betrayer. Imagine. After three years together, they could not discern the change in Judas' heart. Perhaps this happened because they were too focused on their own selfish ambitions rather than on God's plan. Are you so blinded by your own ambition, that you don't understand God's plan?

Our Access to God

One of his disciples, whom Jesus loved, was reclining at table at Jesus' side, so Simon Peter motioned to him to ask Jesus of whom he was speaking.

– JOHN 13:23-24

Read Colossians 3:5-15

When I first began serving the Lord I sought to make a name for myself. I wanted others to see that I was successful. Because I desired the praise of men over the praise of God, I tried to stand out. On one occasion, there was an invitation-only ministry gathering where many important people were in attendance. I thought that if I attended the event, then all these important people would see how influential I was. I contacted some people and finally one of them was able to secure an invitation for me. After the event ended and I had returned home, the Holy Spirit convicted me of my sin. I should have been satisfied knowing that God alone acknowledged me. At that moment, I realized how much I sought the praise of men and was building my ministry with wrong motives.

Several times in the Gospel of John we come across the phrase, "the disciple whom Jesus loved." That disciple's name is never mentioned. John is intentionally expressing that the disciples' name is not of importance. This disciple is satisfied simply by knowing that Jesus loved him. He does not need to stand out. But "the disciple whom Jesus loved" is none other than John himself. With humility, John refuses to write his own name in his gospel so that the focus and glory is on Christ. But, John was not always concerned with the glory of Christ. When he followed Jesus to Jerusalem, John was still trying to secure a throne for himself (Matt. 20:21-24). John had a golden opportunity to promote himself and push aside the other disciples, thereby securing the leadership of the church, when he wrote his gospel account. But something had changed. After Jesus died and rose again, John finally realized that God humbles the proud and lifts up the humble. Now John understood and was living out Jesus' example. That's why he omitted his own name from his gospel.

Take a moment and examine your heart. Are you proud or humble? *When you compare yourself to others, you can appear so willing to serve the Lord. But our comparison is not to one another, it's to Jesus.* Jesus' willingness to wash His disciples' feet and bear our sins on the cross should be reflected by us in serving with humility. There was nothing too humiliating that Jesus was not willing to do for us. At the time that the whole world should have honored and lifted up His name, He was raised up high on a cross and ridiculed. Even when Jesus was mocked and abused, He refused to call down angels to wipe out His enemies. Instead Jesus prayed for them saying, "Father, forgive them, for they know not what they do" (Luke 23:34).

John did not use his status as the "disciple whom Jesus loved" for personal profit either. He was content with being near Jesus. *At any time, with no need for making an appointment or going through an intermediary, John could speak with Jesus. We too can enjoy this same access.* We are children of God. Jesus loves us just as He loved John. If you are struggling with sadness or confusion, you can go right to Jesus. You don't need to schedule a time with Him; He's always available. At every moment and in whatever place you find yourself, Jesus is there to meet you. Praise God that we don't need a mediator to bring us to Jesus. Take advantage of this special privilege—you can go directly to the living Christ anytime you want to. Peter didn't have the courage to ask Jesus directly. Instead, he asked for John's assistance even though he had the same access to Jesus that John did. Don't be timid in bringing your questions and confusions to Jesus. He already knows your thoughts. What is keeping you from using your special privilege to come into Jesus' presence?

Determined to Do God's Will

So that disciple, leaning back against Jesus, said to him, "Lord, who is it?" Jesus answered, "It is he to whom I will give this morsel of bread when I have dipped it." So when he had dipped the morsel, he gave it to Judas, the son of Simon Iscariot.

– JOHN 13:25-26

Read John 7:25-36

God's goals are very often different from our goals. We want immediate answers to the perplexing situations that we find ourselves in. Yet when God answers us immediately, we often don't understand His purposes. Why is it that Jesus often avoids giving a clear response when asked a question? The answer is related to our understanding of God's plan. Oftentimes, we throw questions at God hoping for an immediate answer, so we can move on from our current struggle. But God is working in that situation to accomplish something greater. He is at the same time fulfilling His perfect plan in our lives as well as in the lives of others. For example, the Jewish religious leaders asked Jesus to reveal the source of His authority. Jesus could have plainly answered that He was God Incarnate. An answer like that would have only caused a riot, because the leaders would have accused Jesus of blasphemy. The Pharisees and teachers of the Law were not ready to accept that Jesus was God. Jesus avoided answering directly not because He was afraid to die, He was willing to die, but His death had to be according to the time decreed by the Father.

So, when Jesus announced that one of the disciples would betray Him, His followers grew troubled. This prediction cut to their hearts. One of them was going to hand Jesus over to be killed. How is it possible that someone could be so cruel as to do such a despicable thing? Realizing that, Peter and John, the two disciples nearest to Jesus, wanted to know who Jesus was referring to. We don't know what their motivation was for asking. Perhaps they wanted to beat up the betrayer. That is entirely possible. Or, if Jesus announced it to all the disciples at the table with Him, they might have attempted to prevent the capture of Jesus. Later that night in the garden, Peter attempted to protect Jesus when he pulled out a sword. Whatever the reason, clearly Jesus did not want to reveal the name openly. *We should be impressed by Jesus' determination to go to the cross. Many obstacles stood between Jesus and Golgotha. But at every crossroad, Jesus chose the Father's plan rather than His own well-being.* By not plainly answering John's question, Jesus again chose to deny Himself in order to fulfill the Father's plan.

But in an indirect manner, Jesus did answer John's question. Despite not grasping Jesus' answer at that moment, in God's time John did come to understand it clearly. Has God revealed an answer to you that you found hard to grasp at the time, but later you came to understand? *The important thing is when God answers us, we must obey Him without hesitation.* We obey while waiting for the Lord to fulfill His purpose. Jesus showed John who the betrayer was. He dipped bread in the wine and handed it to Judas. Although Jesus did not announce Judas' name to the disciples, Jesus needed to share the burden of that night with His close friend John. What a blessing it is to have a friend in ministry with whom we can trust our secrets and share our burdens.

Perhaps Jesus didn't tell the other disciples that Judas was the betrayer, because He wanted to give Judas an opportunity to repent. Jesus had already washed Judas' feet and told Judas that He knew of the coming betrayal. Judas was extended one last opportunity to repent. With great patience, the Lord works in the heart of every sinner. As long as the person is still alive, He gives them the opportunity to humble themselves and confess their sin. Never grow weary of offering the gospel to sinners. God is not finished working in their lives. Are you obeying Christ by fulfilling His plans for your life?

Our Gracious God

Then after he had taken the morsel, Satan entered into him. Jesus
said to him, "What you are going to do, do quickly." Now no one at
the table knew why he said this to him. Some thought that, because
Judas had the moneybag, Jesus was telling him, "Buy what we need
for the feast," or that he should give something to the poor.

– JOHN 13:27-29

Read I Corinthians 11:17-34

Judas was sitting at the table with the other disciples.
As the others were inquiring about who would betray Jesus,
Judas joined in asking: "Is it I, Rabbi?" (Matt. 26:25). Judas
already let Jesus wash his feet. He put up a charade by
joining the others in asking who would betray Jesus. Now
he was receiving the bread from Jesus. Judas was such a
hypocrite. More than that, Judas' heart was hardened to the
grace of God. His heart should have broken when Jesus
kneeled before him to wash his feet. He should have been
moved to repentance when he heard Jesus speak about His
betrayal. Jesus' act of love in handing Judas the bread should
have convicted Judas of his sin and brought him to
salvation. *Judas is so faithless. In one night Jesus extended him three*
forms of grace, yet Judas repeatedly rejected that grace.

Once Judas received the bread, Satan sprang into
action. Grace was rejected. Because Judas had hardened his
heart to Jesus, Judas' heart was hardened by God. Now
Judas was Satan's servant. It's sad that God's patience is
considered a sign of weakness by the proud-hearted. Our
hearts are sinful and our actions are evil. When we sin and
discover that God doesn't immediately punish us, we may
feel as though we don't have to worry about sin because it's
no big deal. But, we then proceed to further trod upon the
grace of God. God is patiently waiting for us to repent.
Don't assume that you will always be given another chance
to repent. Many who seem to be so holy are in fact

31

hypocrites. They harden their hearts to the grace of God, and repentance is far from them. Not long after they harden their hearts, they are handed over to Satan.

The Lord's Supper is a serious event. We should keep in mind Paul's words about receiving the Lord's Supper in an unworthy manner (I Cor. 11:27-30). If grace is given through the Lord's Supper, then we should humble ourselves and confess our sins. Paul urges us to "examine yourselves, to see whether you are in the faith" (II Cor. 13:5). Each time we partake in the Lord's Supper, we should first examine our hearts to determine our spiritual health and confess any sins that are dishonoring to the Lord.

When we celebrate the Lord's Supper, we remember that our sins were forgiven at a great price. Jesus gave His life to pay our debt. The wrath of God was poured out on Jesus so that His grace could flow to us. Don't continue to treat sin as an inconsequential thing. You can't deceive or manipulate the Lord. When you receive the bread and wine, remember the humility of Christ who willingly gave Himself as a sacrifice for us so that we might receive His grace.

Judas received bread from Jesus. Jesus then gave the command to Judas to get to work. The plan to betray Jesus was activated. But, the evil actions of Judas would result in the greatest blessing for all mankind. It was time for the Father's plan of salvation to be fulfilled. Although the disciples didn't understand what was happening that night, Jesus knew. He knew that Judas was handed over to Satan. The wicked betrayal of Judas would open the door of heaven for all who believe. It's hard to accept God's plan, but our lack of understanding and the betrayal by evil people cannot keep God's plan from being successfully completed. God is sovereign. Are there sins that you need to confess today?

Disillusionment That Led to Sin

So, after receiving the morsel of bread, he immediately went out.
And it was night.

– JOHN 13:30

Read Matthew 27:1-10

Remembering bad events can be traumatizing. Little things can trigger a memory of that traumatic event. For example, I was very involved in the post-tsunami recovery of Aceh. I saw incredible destruction and smelled the stench of rotting corpses. My heart broke for the Acehnese people who experienced such overwhelming destruction and loss of life. That experience still impacts me today. Every time I am at the beach and see the waves, it triggers the memory I have of the tsunami and affects me deeply. The beautiful waves washing ashore trigger afresh feelings of sorrow that make my heart swell.

The memories of that terrible night were also seared into John's heart. John remembered how Judas rejected Jesus, rose from the table, and disappeared into the night. Judas had been so blessed; how could he do this? He was chosen to serve together with Jesus, after all. Judas witnessed the resurrection of Lazarus firsthand. Like the other disciples, He heard all the teachings of Jesus. But Judas was disillusioned with Jesus. Jesus' plans were different from his plans. Judas wanted to rule from an earthly throne. Jesus was instead willing to hang on a wooden cross. Judas wanted to be the greatest. Jesus was willing to be the lowest. All the blessings that came from serving together with Christ were not enough for Judas. Simply, Judas never submitted to Christ as the Lord of his life. Knowing about or having experiences with Jesus is not enough. Even the evil spirits know who Christ is. *Many know about Jesus, but they refuse to humble themselves before Him.* The work of Jesus should bring us to faith, but, instead, the wicked want to manipulate God for personal gain.

This is not just a problem for worldly people. Judas was not a secular person. He was a disciple who had left his previous occupation to serve the Lord. Yet somewhere along the way Judas grew disillusioned with Jesus because Jesus refused to be crowned king by the crowds. Judas followed Christ for the wrong reasons. He wanted recognition. He wanted to obtain something. But the work of Christ is so much greater than giving a few earthly benefits to Judas and the other disciples. Jesus didn't come to change the world's social system. He came to set the world free from the siege of Satan.

The image of Judas walking out the door stuck in John's memory. Judas departed to do his evil deed. Jesus would not be made king according to Judas' plan. Because of his disappointment, Judas despised Jesus, His teachings, and His sacrifice. Judas ate the bread and then he left. *True disciples put their hopes not in their own plans, but in the Father's will.* When they are humiliated because they do the works that Christ did, they rejoice. Paul was willing to die in prison so that the gospel could be proclaimed. Many other disciples have lived and died in a state of lowliness. They willingly humbled themselves because of the gospel. They put God's plans ahead of their own comforts. Carrying our crosses is not easy—they are heavy. But, as we fix our eyes on Christ and remember His example, He never disappoints those who are faithful to Him.

After Judas left, John wrote that it was night. John clearly remembered the moment when Judas departed from the light of Christ and entered into the darkness. What had already happened in Judas' heart was now happening in the physical world. Darkness covered the soul, heart, and body of Judas. Apart from Jesus, the world is a dangerous place. As long as we stay near to Jesus, we will experience the blessing of His peace. Even in His death, Jesus was filled with peace. As He breathed His last, He proclaimed, "It is finished." His death brought light, but Judas died with regret and in darkness. Are you living to fulfill the Father's will?

Glorifying God

When he had gone out, Jesus said, "Now is the Son of Man glorified, and God is glorified in him. If God is glorified in him, God will also glorify him in himself, and glorify him at once."

– JOHN 13:31-32

Read Romans 5:1-11

Judas departed to sell Jesus to the Jewish religious leaders. In a few hours, Jesus would be crucified. If you knew that you would shortly be betrayed and killed, what would your reaction be? Jesus showed no self-pity like Elijah showed on Mount Horeb. He was not angry like Moses, who struck the rock twice. Jesus was in full control of His emotions. Calmly, He said that the time had finally arrived and that He would now be glorified. Jesus was glorified through Judas' betrayal. This is like the situation that Joseph found himself in when he was sold into slavery in Egypt. After being reunited with his brothers later, Joseph said to them: "You meant evil against me, but God meant it for good" (Gen. 50:20). In all of history, there is no greater evil deed than selling Jesus to His enemies. But God overcame this evil by good—glorifying Jesus.

Jesus rejected the pleas of many who wanted Him to become their earthly king. He knew that the glory of this world is only temporary, but the glory from heaven is eternal. He let Judas work his evil, because through the crucifixion, the glory from heaven would be manifested. Jesus never sought benefits for Himself. He always sought the glory of the Father. *The greatest glory is given to God by all the angels in heaven and the creatures on the earth, because God has redeemed us.* No philosophy, religion, or technology can solve the problem of our separation from God due to sin. People have tried for thousands of years to return to Paradise, but all their efforts have failed. In His death, our problem has been eliminated. Our debt of sin has been paid in full. We can now have fellowship again with a holy God.

Our redemption was planned by God before the creation of the world. The songs of praise in heaven are focused on the fulfillment of God's redemptive plan. The angels rejoice every time a sinner repents. When the church gathers to worship, we confess that the rich and the poor, men and women, the intelligent and the simple, are all redeemed in the same way. God's grace is sufficient to save everyone who believes. No one can add anything to the process of salvation. Everything has been done by God alone. Therefore, all praise and honor and glory is given to God and God alone.

The death of Christ brings glory to Christ and the Father. Jesus told us that He will pay our debt of sin in full. It's easy for someone to promise that. But how can we know that our debt of sin has been paid off? What evidence is there? In order that we might know that the Father accepted Christ's payment for our sins, Jesus rose from the dead. His resurrection proves that Christ didn't die for His own sins. If that was the case, He would not have been able to rise again. This means that Christ is the perfect sacrifice that fulfilled the requirements of the Law. Christ also rose so that we would know that what He promised had been fulfilled. We can have confidence that we have been redeemed. Jesus defeated death. His resurrection is a sign to us that His payment for our sins was accepted. God was glorified in Jesus at the resurrection. Jesus knew that after His death He would rise and ascend to heaven to sit on the throne that was prepared for Him. Heaven is full of glory because Christ has won. He is risen from the dead. Alleluia! The whole earth is full of His glory as the redeemed bring news of that redemption to the uttermost parts of the world. Are you glorifying God by proclaiming the gospel to those who don't yet believe?

Fulfilling Our Part

Little children, yet a little while I am with you. You will seek me, and just as I said to the Jews, so now I also say to you, "Where I am going you cannot come."

– JOHN 13:33

Read John 8:12-30

At the end of their captivity in Egypt, the Israelites gathered their families together to celebrate the Passover. Each family took an unblemished lamb and sacrificed it. The lamb's blood was sprinkled on the doorpost of the house. Then they ate the meat of that lamb. Later that night, the Lord went throughout the entire land of Egypt and killed every firstborn, whether animal or human. Only those who sought refuge in the house under the blood of the lamb that was slain was saved. God commanded the Israelites to commemorate that night by celebrating the Passover every year. The Passover celebration of eating together was God's way to remind Israel that God saves people from their sin. During this meal, parents taught the meaning of the Passover to their children. "And when your children say to you, 'What do you mean by this service?' you shall say, 'It is the sacrifice of the LORD'S Passover, for he passed over the houses of the people of Israel in Egypt, when he struck the Egyptians but spared our houses'" (Ex. 12:26-27).

Jesus celebrated the Passover with His disciples. After Judas departed, Jesus taught them about the meaning of this special Passover when the Lamb of God would be slain to take away the sins of the world. Jesus addressed His disciples as "children." Up until this point, Jesus was their teacher and they were His disciples. Now Jesus was redefining their relationship by calling them "children" and not friends or disciples. Jesus wanted to bring them into the Passover experience. In the same way that a father would teach his children, Jesus taught about the fulfillment of the

Father's plan of salvation. Jesus would return to the Father after suffering a horrible death, so that salvation would be given to us.

Jesus already had told the Jews that He would depart, and they would not find Him anymore. Now Jesus was telling His disciples the same thing. The unbelieving Jews certainly could not go to heaven where Jesus went because they rejected the redemption through Jesus' blood. They continually hardened their hearts and finally rejected Jesus by handing Him over to the Romans. Without the cleansing of sins, no one can enter the presence of God.

Nevertheless, the disciples believed in Christ. They should have been permitted to go where Jesus was going. After Jesus' death and resurrection, the door of heaven would be opened for all who believe in Christ. But in their current state, the disciples could not follow Christ in His death, resurrection, and ascension. *Christ was going to do what no one else could do. He was going to pay our debt of sin. Only Jesus was sinless and could redeem us.* Sinners like us were not qualified to be a mediator between God and men (I Tim. 2:5).

Jesus' disciples were forbidden to follow Jesus to heaven at that moment, because their work on earth was not yet completed. Jesus entrusted them with the task of proclaiming the gospel. There was much to do so that the message of salvation would reach the ends of the earth. Later, there would come a time when they would follow Jesus and go to heaven. At that moment, they had the important responsibility of bearing witness to the death and resurrection of Christ. Jesus had to depart so that the Holy Spirit would come down. If He didn't depart, the disciples would not be able to complete their mission. Even though the disciples wanted Jesus to remain with them, their desires were not Jesus' priority, proclaiming the gospel was the most important concern. Will you commit yourself anew to the task of proclaiming the gospel?

Sacrificial Love

A new commandment I give to you, that you love one another: just as I have loved you, you also are to love one another. By this all people will know that you are my disciples, if you have love for one another.

— JOHN 13:34-35

Read I Corinthians 13:1-13

Solomon wrote, "There is nothing new under the sun" (Eccl. 1:9). Yet Jesus told His disciples that He was giving them a new commandment. By "new" He didn't mean that it was something that was never taught before. The commandment was new in the sense that it was unused or fresh. Remember, Jesus was ministering in the context of the Jewish religion that was dominated by the Pharisees. The Pharisees focused their religious observance on obeying the commands of God. For example, they prioritized the Sabbath Day and considered following this rule as a clear delineation between religious people and sinners. God gave these commands so that we could understand the heart of God, but, instead, the Pharisees focused on the literal meaning of the commands and not the spirit of the commands. They obeyed God's commands, but did so with a cold heart towards God. They were hypocrites.

Obeying God's commands is the obligation of everyone who believes in Christ. Jesus gave us commands that we are expected to obey, but all cold-hearted obedience is rejected by God. Jesus never wanted external obedience alone. The gospel is all about God solving our problem of sin so we can fellowship with Him. Parents want their children to obey them because they love them. So too, in our relationship with God, we obey Him out of our love for Him because we have become children of God.

This command is also new because the love we offer the world reflects the sacrificial love of Christ. Today, the world is experiencing a shortage of love. The kind of love the world sees is often a selfish love that doesn't consider what's best for others. That is not the kind of love we are to show as Christ's disciples. The love of a disciple is based on self-denial and sacrifice. The Father loves the world so much that He gave His only Son so that we could have eternal life and not death. Jesus sacrificed Himself on the cross for us. We are sent out to model the same kind of love to the world. This means that we must be willing to sacrifice ourselves through self-denial.

Throughout His earthly ministry, the love of Jesus was evident. On several occasions, we read that His heart was "moved by compassion" when He saw the sick, the hungry, and the shepherdless. He taught them patiently about the Kingdom of God. He died for their sins. Now we are sent to display His love to the world. Paul wrote that we are "filling up what is lacking in Christ's afflictions for the sake of his body, that is, the church" (Col. 1:24). Paul was willing to leave his community, an example of sacrificial love, to establish the faith of God's children in other places. To further spread the Kingdom of God, every disciple will likewise need to obey the command of Jesus to love one another with the sacrificial love of Christ. With love like this, the world will see Christ and desire to worship Him.

Our love is like our name badge introducing us to the world. There is no place in our lives for anger, hatred, pride, and jealousy. These things are characteristics of the devil and not characteristics of God. God is love. The children of God inherit His character by discarding hatred and pride from their lives and loving others sacrificially. True religion is religion that loves like this. Without exception, to be Christ's disciples, we must love one another. Are you obeying God out of loving gratitude for what He has done for you?

Willing to Die

Simon Peter said to him, "Lord, where are you going?" Jesus answered him, "Where I am going you cannot follow me now, but you will follow afterward." Peter said to him, "Lord, why can I not follow you now? I will lay down my life for you." Jesus answered, "Will you lay down your life for me? Truly, truly, I say to you, the rooster will not crow till you have denied me three times."

– JOHN 13:36-38

Read Mark 14:66-72

Peter often felt like he knew better than everyone else including Jesus. He didn't want to accept Jesus' declaration that he could not go where Jesus was going, so he rebuked Jesus (Matt. 16:22-23) and tried to dictate what Jesus could or could not do (John 13:8). Now, Peter was stubbornly demanding that he be allowed to follow Jesus. His words are a window allowing us to peer into his heart. Someone who doesn't want to listen to those who know more than they do is a person with a heart filled with self-conceit and pride. Peter still hasn't realized that he needs to be quiet in the presence of Jesus. Humble people don't comment before they understand the difficult words they are hearing. Peter certainly struggled with this, and so can we!

Peter did understand one thing: Jesus was talking about His upcoming death. Peter is also willing to die that night. In his mind, he probably wondered why he couldn't die together with Jesus. But, Peter obviously didn't understand the Lord's plans. He didn't know that Jesus would die for sinners, and that later Peter himself would die as a witness to the work of Christ. Peter only continues to think of himself. He was willing to die, but he wanted to die according to *his* plans. Many people make grand boasts using words of great courage. But, courage is not enough. *We need to also have a sensitivity to discern what God is doing at every moment.* Don't, like Peter, think you are so important that

41

you don't need to listen to Jesus' words any longer.

Being willing to die is a declaration that is easy to make, but hard to do. Jesus knew who wanted to sincerely follow Him and who was just pretending to follow Him (Luke 9:57-62). Jesus knew His true followers. He was fully aware that Judas would betray Him. And, He knew that Peter would deny Him three times. Due to his lack of humility, Peter had the wrong estimation of himself.

Instead of denying himself, Peter denied Christ. He did this not only once, but three times! It's so much harder to deny yourself than it is do deny others, because we are all so self-centered. If we find ourselves in a situation that is to our advantage, then we support what is happening. But if we find ourselves in a situation that is to our disadvantage, we quickly find ways to protect ourselves. In a few moments, Jesus would be captured and sent to stand trial. And Peter would be there too. In the courtyard, Peter surveyed the situation and realized there was no hope for freeing Jesus. Moments later, Peter was confronted by people who wanted to connect him with Jesus, but sadly Peter's only concern was to protect himself. (He probably figured that it was already too late to help Jesus, so he should save himself.) Sadly, Peter concluded that it was better for him to deny Jesus than die together with Jesus.

In the end, Peter's boastings of never denying Christ were empty. He vowed to die with Christ, but in the moment of decision he wasn't willing to do so, because he wanted to follow Christ using his own power. That's impossible. *Only the Spirit's supernatural power provides us with the strength to follow Christ in humility and self-denial. It's only through the power of the Holy Spirit that we can give a faithful testimony to Christ.* That is why the disciples were not sent to proclaim the gospel before the Holy Spirit descended upon them. After being filled with the Holy Spirit, however, Peter was finally able to be a witness and lay down his life as a testimony of Christ to the world. Are you willing to lay down your life as a witness?

Facing Difficult Situations

Let not your hearts be troubled. Believe in God; believe also in me.

– JOHN 14:1

Read Mark 4:35-41

When someone departs from home to pursue an adventure, those left behind can be filled with anxiety. When my daughter left for college in another city, I experienced this. What would my daughter's life be like there? Is there a Christian community for her to get involved in? However, my emotions were very different from the emotions that my daughter experienced. She felt, "Finally I am free!" Her heart was filled with peace, self-confidence, and excitement. When Jesus was about to depart, His emotions were quite different from those felt by His disciples. Jesus confronted this great trial with an overwhelming sense of peace. But His disciples were concerned about themselves as they wondered, "What will happen to us?"

Jesus' disciples would be sent into the world to testify to the resurrection. They had spent the past three years in preparation by observing Jesus and being sent out to do ministry (Matt. 10). Now Jesus told them that He would be leaving (John 13:33). This meant that the disciples would have to minister without Christ guiding them. They had every good reason to worry about what was going to happen next. They had grown accustomed to living with Jesus. There was hardly a day that went by that they weren't with Jesus. And when they were apart, the disciples experienced problems like when Jesus sent them across the lake while He went up the mountain to pray all night (Matt. 14:22-24), and a big storm nearly swallowed them up in the sea. Now the disciples found themselves facing another troubling situation—Jesus' bodily departure.

Every Christian who strives to make the gospel known will face difficult situations that will challenge their faith.

There will be times when anxiety fills your heart. But God is near us during those times. We believe what Paul wrote in Philippians 4:6, "do not be anxious about anything, but in everything by prayer and supplication with thanksgiving let your requests be made known to God." *As disciples of Christ, we must believe in Him. We must have confidence in His Word and in His promises.* We can go where He leads us and boldly risk our lives because we are sure of our salvation. Proclaiming the gospel can mean facing persecution from those opposed to God. But God promised He will never leave us and always be with us (Heb. 13:5b).

In the same way that the disciples faced trials, you too may confront dangers. And when you face these dangers without Christ's strength, you do so with great weakness. The disciples served among Jews who opposed their message. Likewise, you may be sent out to places where Christians are few and far between, with many who may oppose you. Perhaps, you are one of the first to believe in Christ, and your community strongly opposes the gospel. As a result, you will find yourself in a weak position, because you are few in number, resources, and influence.

Don't let your heart be troubled. Believe! You will be strengthened by faith. Put your trust in the living God rather than in influential people you may know, your bank account, or even yourself. Only God is worthy of your trust. He will defend, sustain, and protect you. Jesus said, "Believe also in me." The true God is revealed in Jesus Christ alone. He is seated on His throne in heaven ruling all ages. Still today, Jesus is actively serving us. When you find yourself in danger, remember Jesus is with you. His power is active in every situation you are facing – and will face tomorrow – and He will help you overcome the opposition. Have faith. Don't doubt. Don't be paralyzed by fear. Be confident that just as the disciples, who were few in number, could change the world, you too have the same power available to you to overcome obstacles in spreading the gospel through your witness and faithfulness. Are you trusting in God?

Heaven Is Our Home

In my Father's house are many rooms. If it were not so, would I have told you that I go to prepare a place for you?

– JOHN 14:2

Read Revelation 21:1-22:5

Weak on earth; strong in heaven. That is the life of a disciple. We imitate the example of Jesus by humbly carrying our cross so that others will understand the love of God as revealed in the gospel. Even though we are sent out as sheep among wolves, we can trust in Christ because we believe His promises. Although we are proclaiming the gospel out of a position of weakness and without powerful backing on earth, and our rights are often trampled on, all the power of heaven is at our disposal. To all His weak followers, Christ gives this encouragement: "In a little while, I will die. But I know where I am going. I will go to my Father's house. And later you will also die. But you don't need to worry. Because you too will go to my Father's house."

Jesus described heaven for us as His Father's house. Interesting! Most people who want to rest go home—rarely do they go to a strange place to rest. Why do you want to go home when you have a long break? Because home is where your heart is. Jesus is telling His disciples that heaven is not some strange place out there, but is the place where the longings of their hearts will be fulfilled. He says that home is where His Father is. Your heart will be at its greatest peace when you are together with God.

Notice, Jesus doesn't speak of heaven using earthly language. He doesn't describe heaven as a palace with a big river flowing through it. He tells us that it is a place with no more tears. And, it is a place filled with an incredible peace, because in the middle of heaven is God Himself. *Throughout eternity the believers will be in the presence of God. The greatest desire of God's heart is for us to be with Him.* Being in His presence will fill us with overwhelming peace. When Jesus left this world to return to heaven, He left us with a mission: to take the gospel into the whole world. He promised us: "I will be with you always." We are not left alone to carry out His mission. There is nothing that can interfere with our fellowship with Him. We are in His presence for all eternity. This is God's greatest desire. The Father sent the Son to die on the cross to redeem us, and God wants to fellowship with us again.

The Book of Revelation describes heaven as a cube. There is only one other place in the Bible that speaks about a room with the same height, length, and depth. That is the Holy of Holies in the Temple. Once a year the High Priest was allowed to enter, and he was only allowed to enter the Holy of Holies if he brought the blood of a lamb, because God was in that place. Sinful people could never stand before a holy God. Blood had to be brought to cleanse their sins and the sins of the nation.

Because Christ died and returned to the Father, we know that the door of heaven has opened for us. We can now enter heaven—the place of the holy God. We don't have to doubt that we will be received there. Christ has prepared a place for us and has made peace with God for us through His holy blood. In heaven, we can stand before God in full confidence. Finally, we can go home. We can return to the place that we should have been all along. We will be together with God forever. Nothing can take that away from us. Weak believers on earth will have a secure place in heaven no matter what they face now. Our place has been prepared. Jesus has opened heaven for us and He is waiting for us! Have you thanked Christ for making a way for us?

Taking Jesus At His Word

And if I go and prepare a place for you, I will come again and will take you to myself, that where I am you may be also.

— JOHN 14:3

Read Revelation 20:11-15

Believers boldly risk all for Christ because they are certain about what will happen to them after they die. There is no doubt whatsoever. Jesus tells us that He is going to heaven and, while in heaven, He will prepare a place for us. It's not just any old place in heaven, but it's in His Father's house. What an honorable position we have in heaven. Not only is our place personally prepared by Jesus, but it's with the Father and not in some remote corner of Paradise. See how great the Father's love is for us! He has adopted us as His children and not as servants in His heavenly palace.

Our blessings don't end there either. Jesus didn't say that He will prepare a place for us and that we need to gather up enough good works to get us through the front door of His Father's house. He guarantees that we will enter His Father's house, because He will personally bring us there. We enter because of Jesus' work on the cross, not our own. The truth is: we will never have enough good works to bring us to Paradise. Christ has completely paid our debt of sin by His death on the cross. Regardless of how much good works we have accumulated, these works will never be enough to cover our debt of sin before a holy God. *Praise God that entering heaven is not dependent on us. It completely depends on Christ.* He has prepared a place, and He will bring us there. And, we know for sure that we will be accepted when we arrive.

Jesus is personally involved in bringing us to heaven because He wants us there with Him. Many think that heaven is like earth only with greater pleasures. Some religions describe heaven with the riches of this world, because they think that people will follow their religion if they are promised the things that they desired while on earth. What we obtain in heaven is so much greater than all the wealth and pleasures of this world. Our deepest desires will be fulfilled, because our God will be in heaven and we will be together with Him. Everything else pales in comparison.

Jesus promised to bring us to heaven, yet so often we live as though that promise doesn't exist. Sometimes those who believe that they must earn their way to heaven are more diligent in spreading their beliefs than we are. We, who will be brought to heaven by Christ, are given a place of honor in the Father's house, and are adopted as children of God still find our hearts paralyzed by fear. We are afraid to testify that Jesus Christ is Lord. Sadly, even though we have indisputable promises because Christ has risen from the dead, many are still not as courageous as other religions that don't have the certainty of eternal life in heaven.

After we die, there is no guarantee that history will remember us. But Jesus will *never* forget us. God has written our names in the Book of Life, and no name can ever be removed from it. Jesus told us, "I will go to my Father's house." That house is the place where we want to be, because the Father is there. When you put it all in perspective, there is no need to spend a lot of time thinking about your house here on earth. In fact, our earthly house can be an obstacle for entering our heavenly house. Earthly houses can have leaky roofs or be robbed by thieves, but our heavenly house is eternal and secure. When we realize this truth, we should be convinced to live differently so that Christ is glorified through our lives. This is the hope of every believer in Christ: Heaven awaits us so we can serve Christ with confidence. Are you living for heaven or for earth?

Confidence in His Promises

And you know the way to where I am going.

– JOHN 14:4

Read I Kings 17:8-24

Jesus left His disciples to go to heaven because He knew that we would be given all that we needed to continue His mission on earth. One thing that He gave us was the assurance of our salvation: "You know the way to where I am going." *We boldly testify for Christ in spite of the dangers we face, because we are certain of our salvation.* If I was not certain of God's promises, it would be far better for me to prioritize my own comfort. Knowing that I have a great reward in heaven, I don't need to seek riches on earth. For people who don't have the certainty of heaven, when they die, it would be better for them to just stay in their house because the world is a dangerous place. There are car accidents, plane crashes, murders, and the list goes on. If you aren't convinced that your life is in God's hands, then it's best to just play it safe and stay home. When God calls me to heaven, I know I will go straight to the Father's House. What a comfort that is for the believer.

Because of His promises, I am willing to attempt what many deem as impossible for God's glory. He has promised that His Word would not return to Him empty (Isa. 55:11); He has promised that He will send us out and be with us, to name a few. Therefore, I boldly proclaim the gospel because I know that it is not I who work, but God who is working through me to bring people to faith. We can be daring in our faith because of the promises of God. To be faithful in ministry, we must be willing to risk our lives based on His promises.

It's not only our own lives that are at risk, but also our families. As a parent, I know what it's like to struggle with worry over my children. I want them to be safe just as I trust God to provide for my needs and keep me safe. It's easy for me to trust God with my life, but difficult for me to trust Him with my children's needs. If God is leading my life, why can't I trust that He is also leading the lives of my children? Likewise, we can also struggle to believe that God will faithfully take care of our disciples. Remember, the Holy Spirit that is in your life is also in the lives of your disciples. He is present to the same degree with the same power. It can be easy to doubt God's love and care. But our worries over our children's or disciples' futures means we're not fully trusting God. God wants us to trust Him with every concern of our heart.

Don't limit your faith only to yourself. You can be confident that God's promises will extend not only to your own life, but also to the lives of other believers. Wanting to help a fellow believer is commendable. So, when you see people in difficulty, you should have compassion for them just as Jesus does. In fact, by doing so, you could be God's answer to their prayers as you meet their needs. But you will also need to be praying for wisdom. Sometimes God is using a situation in their lives to strengthen their faith so that they learn to trust in God's promises. In that case, you want to be careful not to be too quick to step in and short-circuit God's work in their lives. The Spirit will lead you as you seek Him. For example, a person needing help may think that "If only I had more money, then I wouldn't have any problems." If that were the case, God would have put an ATM machine with an unlimited supply of free money in every church. But He didn't. The solution for that person is to seek God, discover His will, and trust in His provisions for them. It's the task of every disciple to learn to trust and depend on God alone so that their faith will grow. And, by doing so, they will be ready to do greater works for God. What are God's promises and are you believing in them?

Trust in God

Thomas said to him, "Lord, we do not know where you are going.
How can we know the way?"

– JOHN 14:5

Read Hebrews 11:1-40

Everybody knows the way to their parents' house. I remember when I was young, our family would visit my father's village. Even though we were still far from the village, my father would tell us that it was only eight more turns until we arrived at my grandparent's house. After eight turns and 30 minutes, we would indeed arrive. Jesus returned to His Father's house. He knew the way too. If His disciples were told to return to their homes, they would also know the way back to their villages without any difficulties. But Jesus was not going to the homes of His disciples; He was going to His Father's house. Jesus' statement about going to His Father's house to prepare a place for them should have given them confidence. Instead, it only added to their restlessness. The disciples had no idea how to get there. You can almost feel the sense of panic in Thomas' question.

As followers of Christ, we must live by faith. There is no other way. *Those willing to serve Christ with humility and self-denial do so, because they believe that everything will happen just as Jesus said it would.* Every day we go out into a sinful world that rejects the gospel. It's easy for us to grow weary and become discouraged. At our weakest moments, Satan is there to tempt us to doubt the promises of God. That is what Satan did with Adam and Eve in the Garden of Eden. He told them, "You will not surely die. For God knows that when you eat of it your eyes will be opened, and you will be like God, knowing good and evil" (Gen 3:4-5). The Devil planted doubt in Adam and Eve's hearts so they would not trust God's Word, and in the end, they chose to go against God's will.

51

Now Thomas was panicking. He didn't want Jesus to go. But if Jesus didn't go, the Holy Spirit wouldn't have come down to us. Jesus had to depart, because it was God's will. Thomas could only think of himself at this time. The disciples should be coming alongside Jesus and strengthening Him as He prepared for death on the cross, but they failed to do so. Instead, they sought to only take care of themselves. It's disappointing to see how little they understood God's will and how little they were willing to trust the Father. Jesus was full of peace as He faced the cross, because He was confident in the Father's plan.

You have been sent by Christ to be His witness, and Satan knows that many will believe in Christ because of your testimony. *Satan is diligently working to destroy your ministry, and one of his most effective weapons is to keep you from focusing on heaven by making you think this world is most important.* Since the beginning, the Devil has been destroying God's work. Every time you hear Satan say that you should not seek first the Kingdom of God and only take care of yourself, you need to return to God's Word and be confident that all He has promised will certainly happen. Don't let your emotions guide your heart. Our emotions must be overcome with God's Word. Every day we must choose God and not the Devil.

Scripture tells us many things: don't let your heart be troubled; believe in Jesus; He is going to the Father's house; He will come back again to take us to Heaven; Jesus paid the price to get us there; you will go directly into God's eternal presence—and you can confidently carry out your ministry based on these promises. As you abide with Christ, you will better understand what God's will is for your life. If you believe in Him and all His promises, you will be able to face your ministry challenges without a troubled heart. Today, you are facing an important choice: Will you trust God and faithfully serve Him, or will you let Satan prevent you from doing God's will?

Jesus Is the Only Solution

Jesus said to him, "I am the way, and the truth, and the life. No one comes to the Father except through me."

— JOHN 14:6

Read Colossians 2:8-15

God created us to live eternally with Him in deep fellowship so that we might know Him and His will. But sin ruined all of that. It separated us from God, threw us into confusion, and brought death. On this evening, the disciples were facing a similar situation. They were about to be separated from Christ. Their hearts were distressed because they wanted to be with Him. This was a great problem for them. In fact, it is *the* problem. We have tried in various ways to overcome this problem, but nothing works. Sin has alienated us from God. Because of sin, we no longer know Him and what His will is. Instead, death reigns over us.

Jesus, however, provides us the way out of this dilemma. He says, "I am the way, the truth, and the life. No one comes to the Father except through me." What an astounding statement! Jesus tells His disciples that our alienation with God is solved because He is *the* Way to God. We can know God because Jesus is *the* Truth incarnate. Death has been defeated, because Jesus is *the* Life for all who believe. Only Jesus can solve our greatest problem. No person or philosophy can ever solve even part of the problem. Jesus completely solved it when He paid the debt for our sin. As we reflect on this, *we should grow in certainty that the gospel must be proclaimed to all since only Jesus is* the *answer to* the *problem.*

Some people might react negatively to Jesus,' claim saying that He is arrogant. Other religions also claim to offer a way to God. We can confuse respect for other religions with whether or not their teaching is true. Any religion that doesn't solve our biggest problem is not worthy of being followed. In the end, everyone will be confronted by Jesus' claim and must wrestle with the question: Is He the *only* way to the Father? Other religions have their opinions of Jesus. Many respect Him. Muslims believe Jesus was a prophet. Hindus view Jesus as a wise and holy teacher. Even Atheists, who deny that God exists, say they still admire Jesus' ethical teachings. But, Jesus is different from all other religious leaders.

Other religious leaders offer us a set of rules, a mystical experience, or special knowledge that is supposed to change our lives. Jesus did not give us new things to do. He gave us *Himself.* Knowledge and rules are not the way to God. Only through Christ's death and resurrection is the door to heaven open to us. *Jesus solved our problem.* Do you believe that? Sin was defeated, because of what Jesus did for us. We have been set free from the crushing debt that has enslaved us. Now we can enjoy our fellowship with God again, because God did what no one else could do—He paid our debt.

In light of this reality, we should give ourselves fully to the work of the gospel. There is no other hope for our family, friends, and acquaintances. They can only find eternal life through Christ. The saddest reality is that the door of heaven is open, but people have yet to hear about God's redemption for them. That's why God is sending us into the broken and dying world with this message. Who do you need to share the gospel with today?

Knowing Christ

If you had known me, you would have known my Father also. From now on you do know him and have seen him.

– JOHN 14:7

Read Luke 24:13-35

A man once came to my house. For a long time he had searched for God. He diligently performed his religious obligations and attended prayers. He spent many hours reading his holy book, but he never felt that God cared about him. After he heard the gospel, he received Christ in his heart. He then announced, "Now God is in my heart. I am full of peace." He realized that experiencing God was only possible through Christ.

Religions offer God to their adherents and say if you follow their teachings or meditate on their life principles, then you can find God. But, as believers, we know that it's not possible to know God through our own thoughts or works. Our thoughts can deceive us, because they are too easily corrupted by sin, and we are blinded by the gods of this age (II Cor. 4:4). *We don't have the capacity to see God. The one and only way to know God is for Him to shine into our dark minds.*

Some people are very diligent in studying religion. They can even major in religious studies at the university. A person can be very academically knowledgeable about religion, but knowledge about a religion doesn't mean you *know* God. Knowledge can help you pass an exam, but it will not help you enter Paradise. Even the demons knew about Jesus, but didn't worship Him (Mark 5:7-8). Knowing is different from knowing about. *Knowing* implies two parties having a growing, intimate relationship with one another. Knowing God, then, goes beyond only having an intellectual understanding about God; it means developing a *personal* relationship with Him. This relationship is based on humility, because we submit to what is revealed to us in

God's Word. And, we prove our submission by enthusiastically obeying His commands.

Submission is difficult because we can find ourselves rejecting what is revealed in the Scriptures. Jesus said that knowing the Father is only possible through believing in Christ. Initially, when people first hear Jesus' words and are amazed at His miracles, they are attracted to Christ. This was the case with many of Jesus' disciples. They followed Jesus without fully comprehending who He was. But after they met the risen Christ, they believed that Jesus is Lord. That was a dramatic change in their beliefs. Throughout their lives, the disciples believed that God was only in heaven. After seeing the resurrected Christ, they finally understood that God became flesh so that He could pay the penalty for their sins. Amazingly, the Almighty God entered time and space to redeem us. Although it was difficult to understand that God could become a man, this is what He did. And because God revealed it, it can't be wrong.

Truth stands above all else. It never bows to anyone including a king. We are the ones who must bow before the truth. If you desire to know God personally, then you must believe in Jesus, the Lord. Because He has redeemed us through His death, we can have fellowship with God as His children. This is a certainty. If we know Jesus, then we know the Father. God is no longer hidden by our dark hearts. Our hearts and minds have been renewed, and we can now see God. Today, God is revealing Himself to many people. He is showing them that Jesus is Lord. For those who will humble themselves and accept Christ into their hearts, they will see God. What does God's Word reveal to you about who Jesus is?

Seeing the Father Through Christ

Philip said to him, "Lord, show us the Father, and it is enough for
us." Jesus said to him, "Have I been with you so long, and you still do
not know me, Philip? Whoever has seen me has seen the Father.
How can you say, 'Show us the Father'"?

– JOHN 14:8-9

Read Exodus 33:12-34:9

Philip was confused. Jesus told him that he had already
seen the Father and now knows Him. But Philip didn't feel
as though he had seen God, and he wanted so badly to know
the Father. In fact, it was the deepest longing of his heart.
He knew that he would not be complete unless God was
dwelling in his heart in perfect fellowship. Whenever Philip
was together with Jesus, Philip felt fulfilled. So, he wanted
to stay near to Jesus. But Jesus was going to leave soon.
Philip knew that Jesus' departure would devastate him, so
he wanted to make sure that he at least had the Father.

Philip's exclamation, "Lord, show us the Father, and it
is enough for us," reveals a great truth. Having the Father is
enough. When you have Him, you have all the blessings in
the heavenly places. For years, the disciples had watched
Jesus as He healed the sick, cast out demons, and taught the
lost sheep of Israel. Philip and the other disciples would
now be asked to continue that work. To do so, they would
need what Jesus had. *Finally, Philip understood that everything*
that Jesus had was found in His relationship with the Father. If
Philip could only see the Father, he would have all that he
would need, too.

The history of Israel in the Old Testament is full of
men and women used by God. In all of Israel there perhaps
was none greater than Moses. One important thing
differentiated Moses from all the other great men and
women of Israel. God said that He spoke face-to-face with
Moses. To all the other people, He spoke only through

mediators. Moses had a special relationship with God. He met God on Mount Sinai, and God made His glory pass before Moses. He proclaimed His name, "The Lord, the Lord, a God merciful and gracious, slow to anger, and abounding in steadfast love and faithfulness" (Ex. 34:6). Moses was unable to lead the people of Israel until He had seen God's glory.

Philip knew that seeing God's glory for even a short moment would be enough. Then, like Moses, he would be able to do the work that Christ was commissioning him to do. He would have the power that Jesus had to serve God. But Philip's request showed that he didn't yet know Jesus nor the Father. It was all there in front of him: Philip was standing in the presence of Jesus, God's glory was in his midst, yet Philip was unaware.

Jesus announced with great clarity that He was God: "Whoever has seen me has seen the Father." Seeing Christ in His glory is the same as seeing the Father. The Father and Jesus are one. Jesus' announcement has revealed for us the truth of heaven. Christ is enough for us to know and see God, for the fullness of God dwells in Him (Col. 1:19). Jesus *is* God. That is why John states, "And the Word became flesh and dwelt among us, and we have seen his glory, glory as of the only Son from the Father, full of grace and truth" (John 1:14). The glory of God that met Moses on Mount Sinai and filled the Temple in Jerusalem is in Jesus. If you believe in Christ, you too will have seen God's glory. How do you see the glory of God in the Son?

Believe His Works

Do you not believe that I am in the Father and the Father is in me?
The words that I say to you I do not speak on my own authority, but
the Father who dwells in me does his works. Believe me that I am in
the Father and the Father is in me, or else believe on account of the
works themselves.

– JOHN 14:10-11

Read John 10:22-40

Jesus has made an outstanding claim: "Whoever has seen me has seen the Father." He has revealed plainly His deity. Jesus Christ is Lord. It's often hard when someone hears that Jesus is God for the first time, because throughout their whole lives they have been told that Jesus is not God. Yet throughout His ministry, Jesus did only that which God can do: He raised the dead; knew people's thoughts; and forgave sins. This was not done with magic, but simply by speaking a word. Looking at these works and understanding Jesus' claim leaves each of us with a decision to make. *Will you believe?* No one can stay neutral in relationship to Christ. He is either God or He is not. Every person must decide what they believe.

Fortunately, God didn't leave us to make our decision without any evidence. Jesus tells us that His proclamation of His deity didn't originate from Himself, but from the Father. When Jesus performed miracles, taught, and forgave sins, He was not working alone but together with the Father. This is the secret of the Trinity. The Trinity is not three Gods, but one. *The Trinity is a unity—one voice and one action working together to bring the maximum glory to God through fulfilling God's plan of redemption.* No one's mind can grasp the secrets of God, but we can understand that the Trinity is a unity. The Trinity cannot be understood by our own logic.

Jesus knew that the revelation of God's being would be hard for us to understand so He directed us to examine

59

the evidence: "Believe on account of the works themselves." Jesus desires for us to look at all the works that the Father and the Son did together. The phrase "the works that I do" is also found in John 10:25. Jesus said, "I told you, and you do not believe. The works that I do in my Father's name bear witness about me." Any honest examination will lead to the conclusion that Jesus is Lord. Jesus is saying that we should let His works lead us to faith.

On one occasion, I was sharing the gospel with someone who had changed His religion several times, because he wanted to find a religion that was in accordance to what he thought was true. He didn't accept that we were polluted by Adam's sin, because He believed that Adam already paid the penalty for his own sin. This man also could not accept the Trinity. As I was sharing the gospel with him, I pointed him to the works that Jesus did. Ultimately, I pointed him to Jesus' crowning work of dying on the cross and rising again. This is the work that proves that Jesus is Lord, because only God could redeem us. No one else would qualify as payment for our sins. The proof of the resurrection is great. Even history can't dispute it. Paul wrote of the resurrection, stating that if you didn't believe what he was saying, you could ask some of the 500 eyewitnesses, many of whom were still alive when Paul was writing (I Cor. 15:6).

Jesus didn't say that we should believe because God fits with our assumptions and worldview. He said we should believe because He told us the truth and proved it with His works. His works testify to all people through all ages. Jesus Christ is Lord. What conclusion are you drawing from the works that Christ did?

Doing Jesus' Works

Truly, truly, I say to you, whoever believes in me will also do the works that I do...

– JOHN 14:12a

Read II Corinthians 5:11-21

Jesus came to fulfill God's plan of salvation through His death on the cross and His resurrection. Once the plan was fulfilled, it was entrusted to every one of His followers to be proclaimed. This plan was so great that it would not only be the responsibility of a privileged few, but Jesus called and sent out every one of us who believes to do the works that He does. The phrase "whoever believes in me" appears several times in the Gospel of John. For example, Jesus says: "Whoever believes in me, though he die, yet shall he live" (John 11:25). Here Jesus means every believer since eternal life is for all who believe. This phrase also occurs in in John 6:35, 7:38, and 12:46. Clearly, Jesus uses this phrase to mean every believer, not just those who are His disciples or leaders of the church.

When Jesus tells us that "whoever believes in me will also do the works that I do," He is describing the *normal Christian life*. Everyone who believes should be doing what Jesus was doing. If that is the case, then we need to answer an important question: What were the works that Jesus did? Up to this point in the Book of John, Jesus performed many miracles such as turning water into wine (John 2:1–11), healing a man who was crippled for 38 years (John 5:1–9); feeding 5,000 people with five loaves and two fish (John 6:1–14), and raising Lazarus from the dead (John 11:43–44). When Jesus tells us that every believer will do the works that He does, should we assume that we will also do all these things? If that is the case, then we are in big trouble. I have never raised the dead or healed a cripple. I haven't even done the easiest one of turning water into wine!

Focusing on the miracles of Jesus can distract us from

the real meaning of Jesus' words. Jesus' works were meant to point people to the truth of who He is so they worship Him as their Savior and Lord. *All of Jesus' works, both the amazing, miraculous ones as well as the simple ones, were to show the lost world that Jesus is Lord. In the same way, all your works should also testify to those lost in sin that Jesus has come to save them.* God has asked us to disperse into the various countries and communities of the world to testify that the Father, through the Son, has reconciled the world to Himself. We are sent out as Ambassadors for Christ to make known the love of Christ to those who are still opposing God. We are to speak His words and live a life of testimony consistent with who our King is.

The way you trust God for your marriage, finances, and health should show the world that you serve a Risen Savior. Everything that you say and do should reflect your full confidence in Christ for your life in this world and the next. It's your works that display the trustworthiness of Jesus. Jesus said, "Let your light shine before others, so that they may see your good works and give glory to your Father who is in heaven" (Matt. 5:16). The world is watching you. They want to see if Jesus is who He says He is. They want to know if Jesus can be trusted. The world must hear the news of salvation through Christ.

The work that we are to do is to show the world that Jesus is Savior and Lord. Sadly, many things in our lives do not testify to that fact. Perhaps there is something in your life that is not consistent with your faith in Christ. Don't delay to confess your sins to God, so He will restore you to Himself, and you can continue proclaiming Christ to the world. How are you doing the work that Jesus did?

Greater Works

...and greater works than these will he do, because I am going to the Father.

— JOHN 14:12b

Read John 12:20-50

Jesus didn't just commission every believer to be His witness by doing the works that He did; He also sent us out to do greater works than He did. This is truly amazing. I would be satisfied to do what Jesus did, but God wants more for us. He wants us to do even greater works but greater works doesn't necessarily mean more miraculous. I don't know of a single person, apart from Christ, who has fed 5,000 people with five loaves of bread and two fish. And, I have never heard of a single Christian who has walked on water. If we have not done even these things, we certainly cannot do something greater.

Remember that the works that Jesus did was to testify that the Son came from the Father to offer Himself as our atoning sacrifice. We do the works that Jesus did when we testify to this truth. So, the greater works that we do is to give a greater testimony to Jesus as Savior and Lord. There are two ways that every believer does greater works than Jesus did. The first way is found in the content of the gospel message that we proclaim, and the second way is found in the scope that the message is proclaimed. *Believers are given a greater gospel to proclaim in the sense that it's now a message of completed redemption, rather than of promised redemption.* Until the death of Christ, the world only had *hope* that someday the Messiah would come to take away their sins. The Jews were commanded by God to institute daily sacrifices for their sin. Once a year, the High Priest was to bring the blood of an unblemished sheep into the Most Holy Place where God's glory dwelt. This was to be a reminder that, without the shedding of blood, there would be no forgiveness of sins. All of these sacrifices pointed to a day in the future when the Lamb of God would take away the sins of the world.

Now, Jesus is speaking to His disciples on the night before His crucifixion. He has not yet shed His blood for the forgiveness of their sins, so the message that Jesus proclaimed that night was still a gospel of the promised sacrifice. Soon, all that was to change. In one day's time, with blood running down His head, hands, and feet, Jesus will proclaim, "It is finished." As a result, atonement has been made for our sins. Our debt has been paid. We are now sent into the world to perform greater works by testifying to the completed gospel and a paid ransom.

There is another way we can do greater works. Jesus sent us out to proclaim this gospel message throughout the entire world. For Jesus, He rarely ventured outside the borders of Israel. In fact, almost His entire ministry was spent among the Jewish people, "I was sent only to the lost sheep of the house of Israel" (Matt. 15:24). Jesus' mission was to complete the Father's plan of salvation by fulfilling all that was prophesied about Him in the Old Testament. And Jesus fulfilled hundreds of prophecies concerning His birth, life, death, and resurrection. That is why He rarely ministered to those who were not Jews. It wasn't until the week of His crucifixion that He spoke to a delegation of Greeks. Jesus received them because "the hour has come for the Son of Man to be glorified" (John 12:23).

Jesus never proclaimed the Good News in Rome. He never healed people in Tokyo. He never taught in Moscow. But His followers have. And we must continue to do so. Many are still waiting to hear the Good News. Every believer is to do greater works by going to places that Jesus never went and proclaiming salvation through Jesus' name. Jesus sends us to the whole world. Where is He sending you to proclaim the gospel?

Praying for Greater Works

Whatever you ask in my name, this I will do, that the Father may be glorified in the Son. If you ask me anything in my name, I will do it.

— JOHN 14:13-14

Read Acts 4:23-31

What have you prayed for today? Was it something for yourself or your family? Certainly, we should pray for those things. In Jesus' teaching on prayer, we are told to pray for our daily bread (Matt. 6:9-13). In addition to that, Jesus wants us to pray for something even more important. He wants us to pray that God's name would be glorified throughout the world. Our first priority in prayer is to glorify God, because there are so many places where God's name is not honored. In fact, today many continue to defame His name in their religious practices or in the media. If we have experienced God's love in our lives because we have found forgiveness of sins in Christ, it should be our desire for other sinners to find that love as well. God's love should change the content of our prayers.

Jesus tells us that we will do greater works. In order to do these greater works, however, we need a power that is greater than what we have in ourselves. After commissioning us to do greater works, Jesus immediately gives all believers the resources to do those works. He doesn't want us to serve Him with frustration and weariness. When Jesus went to the Father, it was so the Holy Spirit would come. It is the Holy Spirit and His power that will perform these greater works through us. He will draw men and women to Himself through the gospel that we proclaim. Our words are nothing unless they are accompanied by the Spirit's to change people's hard hearts, so that they will receive salvation through Christ.

When we pray that the Father will be glorified through Jesus, we are unleashing the Holy Spirit's power through our testimony. *Everything we need to do these greater works has already been provided and is accessed through prayer.* This is exactly what Jesus promised us when He said, "Whatever you ask in my name, this I will do." He put no conditions on this request. However, when we pray for ourselves, God places conditions on those prayers. Jesus teaches in John 15:7 that, "If you abide in me, and my words abide in you, ask whatever you wish, and it will be done for you." Answered prayers are always a result of being in line with God's will. The Apostle John echoes this when he writes, "If we ask anything according to his will he hears us. And if we know that he hears us in whatever we ask, we know that we have the requests that we have asked of him" (I John 5:14-15). But when we pray that our greater works will point to Christ, there are no conditions for answering those prayers. God *will* respond for the sake of His own glory.

Prayer is the key to unleashing the power of the Holy Spirit through our testimony. And God is most glorified when sinners repent. Even the angels of heaven shout for joy; so pray that the Father will be gloried in the Son. Pray that God will use your life to testify boldly on His behalf. Spend some time today asking God to draw your family, friends, and neighbors to faith in Christ. It is God's desire that all should believe (I Tim. 2:3-4). And, God is drawing many to Himself. As you share the gospel with the lost, God's Spirit will work in their hearts to bring them to faith in Christ. What will you pray for today?

Obeying His Commandments

If you love me, you will keep my commandments.

– JOHN 14:15

Read Luke 7:36-50

Our relationship with Christ began the moment we received Him into our hearts as Savior and Lord. In this moment, we made a covenant with Him. We accepted the fact that we could not redeem ourselves and trusted Christ's works as the basis for our salvation. We confessed that He is our Savior. But we also accepted that He is our Lord. Savior and Lord is a package. We cannot have one without the other. If Jesus is not God, then He was not qualified to save us. If Jesus is not a Savior, then He is not loving, which is the very nature of God. Many of us today, however, only want Jesus as Savior without having Jesus as Lord. We want the certainty of heaven, while keeping control over our lives on earth. Unfortunately, that is not God's plan.

If we truly love Christ and have accepted Him as our Savior, our entire life's orientation will change. We will no longer be thinking of how we can gain advantage for ourselves. *Knowing the great debt that God paid by forgiving us will cause our hearts to overflow with gratitude. As His humble servants, we will desire to obey His every command.* The greatest desire of our heart will be to please God through obedience to Him. In the Scriptures, God has given us clear commands. He has told us that our covenant with Him means that we will reflect His glory to all the nations by obeying Him. The commandments are meant to be easy and not a burden. Jesus tells us, "Take my yoke upon you, and learn from me, for I am gentle and lowly in heart, and you will find rest for your souls" (Matt. 11:29). Following Christ means conforming to His will, and only then will our souls find rest.

The commands that Jesus gave can be categorized into seven general groups: 1. Repent, believe, and receive the

Holy Spirit (Mark 1:15; John 20:22); 2. Be baptized (Matt. 28:18-20); 3. Celebrate the Lord's Supper (Luke 22:19-20); 4. Love God and one another (Mark 12:29-31); 5. Pray (John 16:24); 6. Give (Luke 6:38); and 7. Make disciples (Matt. 28:18-20; Acts 1:8; John 21:15-17). These seven groups of commandments reflect the very work of Christ, which is to fulfill the Father's plan of salvation. When we respond to that salvation by declaring our love for God, it initiates a relationship with Him where all who believe will do the work that He does. As a response to our salvation, we obey God by immersing ourselves into the work of salvation, and we proclaim the gospel to those who have yet to receive Him. These commandments are oriented around that reality. The more we love Christ, the more we want to obey Him by doing His works and following His teachings.

We obey the command of the Great Commission to make disciples. This results in people repenting and believing in Christ. Then, they confess that to God and the world through their baptism and participation in the Lord's Supper. Additionally, they proclaim it to the world by loving God more than money and loving others as they love themselves. This love works continually in their hearts, so they realize that others need this salvation. They pray and give to make that happen.

Your obedience to Christ's commandments is a key to changing the world. Too many people claim to follow Christ, but only want the benefits of a relationship with Him without submitting to His Lordship. Oftentimes, that's why the church has so little impact on the world. Many have chosen to only believe because it's advantageous to themselves, rather than thinking what is most important to bring glory to God. Which of Christ's commandments do you need to obey?

The Power to Obey

And I will ask the Father, and he will give you another Helper, to be with you forever, even the Spirit of truth, whom the world cannot receive, because it neither sees him nor knows him. You know him, for he dwells with you and will be in you.

– JOHN 14:16-17

Read Romans 7:14-8:2

We desire to obey God's commands, but too often we are weak and fail when we try using our own strength. Our flesh continues to wage war against our heart's desire to obey God, and we simply can't succeed. Thankfully, God doesn't leave us alone in our desperation. He gives us the gift of the Holy Spirit, so that we can live our life in obedience to God. Jesus Himself asked the Father to send the Holy Spirit. He knew that without the Spirit, it would be impossible for us to obey the command to do the work that He did.

Try to imagine the difficulties the disciples faced after Jesus rose from the dead. Jesus sent them into all the world to proclaim the news of the resurrection. He gave them a vision, but didn't provide them with any of the resources needed to fulfill that vision; resources like transportation, funds, or even an organization. From a worldly perspective, Jesus didn't equip them with what was needed. And to top it all off, they weren't sent into friendly areas, but to places fraught with danger. However, Jesus knew a Helper was coming—the Holy Spirit. Jesus' presence through the indwelling of the Holy Spirit would be enough. Every other worldly preparation would pale in comparison to His presence. With the Holy Spirit, they had all they needed to fulfill God's plan.

The Holy Spirit is of utmost importance in the life of every believer. He is *all* that we need. The world doesn't have the Holy Spirit, because the Spirit is holy. He can't dwell in those who are unholy. Unless the heart is cleansed by the blood of Christ, we are not qualified to be the temple of the Holy Spirit. The world has rejected Christ, so they are still contaminated by their sin and worldly passions. *But even the weakest believers have been cleansed and given the power to obey the commands of Christ to do His works.* The Holy Spirit resides in each of us to turn this world upside down for Christ. Instead of putting us in a situation where our hearts are filled with discouragement, because we face an impossible task, God has filled our hearts with Himself. Through the Holy Spirit, He is with us until the end of the age.

Jesus refers to the Holy Spirit as the Spirit of Truth. That's because our message to the world is *true*. It's very important that our lives reflect holy living, so that our lives and our message are in sync. The Pharisees were some of Jesus' biggest opponents. They were the religious leaders who, on the outside, appeared to obey God's commands, but their hearts were far from Him. Jesus calls them hypocrites. Their hypocrisy led them to opposing Christ and working to have Him crucified. We, too, are in danger of becoming hypocrites. The Spirit of Truth has been given to us so that we understand what is true about God and have the power to live according to that truth. This enables us to give a true testimony, rather than hypocritical, about Christ.

The Holy Spirit has been given as a helper to us. He leads us in the truth about Christ and the truth about ourselves. He changes our sinful hearts by purifying them for God. The Spirit of Truth will help us live lives of self-denial and humility—and to be good witnesses for Christ. It's the Holy Spirit who changes our minds and hearts to understand who we are in relation to the true God. Are you using the power of the Holy Spirit in your life to do the works that Christ did?

Focusing on The Greater Works

I will not leave you as orphans; I will come to you. Yet a little while and the world will see me no more, but you will see me. Because I live, you also will live.

– JOHN 14:18-19

Read Acts 18:1-17

If we are convinced that Jesus is with us and that we will live after we die, then we will boldly strive to make His name known. As we grow in Christ, the temptations of this world will lose their power, and we will do greater works because we know that our future is in the Lord's hands. *People who do great things for God are those who don't put their own considerations first.* We reject the temptations of this world because we know that God is worthy to be worshipped by all people. We die to ourselves by denying our ambitions and prioritizing the things of God.

Paul is an example of someone who denied himself. He had one of the most interesting conversions in Scripture, and was used by God in amazing ways. Paul didn't focus on his future, because he knew that Jesus was with him and that he would live again. On one of his ministry journeys, Paul left Timothy in Macedonia and went on alone to Athens to proclaim the gospel. After he finished his ministry in Athens, Paul departed for Corinth. Why did Paul continue his journey to Corinth rather than wait for Timothy to join him in Athens? The distance from Athens to Corinth was approximately only 60 kilometers. More importantly, Athens faced the east, being located on the Aegean Sea, and Corinth faced west, being located on the Ionian Sea. Many ships would unload their cargo in the harbor near Athens and bring the goods overland to Corinth, where they would be loaded on ships headed to Rome. This route saved shippers much time and money.

When Paul was called to be an apostle, the Lord

commissioned him to testify before Caesar in Rome. While he was proclaiming the gospel in other regions, Paul's eyes were constantly focused on Rome. He never forgot that he was to go to Rome to proclaim the gospel and defend all Christians before Caesar. Corinth was not too far from Rome. Perhaps Paul thought, if he could get to Corinth, then he could find a ship sailing to Rome. When he arrived in Corinth, Paul worked making tents. On the Sabbath, he went into the synagogue and taught about Christ. This means that all week-long Paul worked and only did ministry one day a week. But once Timothy and Silas arrived from Macedonia, Paul stopped making tents. Timothy and Silas worked, while Paul proclaimed the gospel every day.

Paul made tents while in Corinth because he needed the money since very few people supported his ministry. When Paul arrived in Corinth, he was poor and alone. He walked from place to place, because it cost money to go by boat, but walking was free. Yet, Paul never wrote a letter to Peter saying, "Hey, how come you never send me any money?" Paul knew that the believers from Jewish backgrounds had become refugees after being expelled from Jerusalem. By faith, Paul trusted in Christ and didn't complain. He knew that he would not be orphaned by God.

Notice the sacrifice of Paul, who was willing to do the greater works that Jesus called him to, instead of seeking worldly things. Paul's focus remained only on proclaiming the gospel. He courageously faced trials, because he knew that even if he died, he would live again. God defended Paul just as He promised He would. Why are you serving the Lord? Many serve because they are guaranteed certain benefits or are seeking fame, but that shouldn't be the motivation for our service. Remember, the Helper will be with you wherever He calls you to serve Him. What are you willing to sacrifice in order to do the greater works?

Union with Christ

In that day you will know that I am in my Father, and you in me,
and I in you.

— JOHN 14:20

Read Ephesians 1:1-14

Jesus' desire for all believers is that we do greater works than He did. After proclaiming this amazing vision for our lives, Jesus went on to explain how that will happen. We will do these works when we ask in prayer (vs. 13-14), obey His commandments (v. 15), depend on the Holy Spirit (vs. 16-17), and live in union with Christ (vs. 18-20). Being *in* Christ is essential to the Christian life. In just a few more verses, Jesus will refer to this as abiding in Him, saying that He is the vine and we are the branches (John 15:1-6).

The Father and Son are in perfect union with one another. Throughout his gospel, John emphasizes the unity of the Son and the Father (John 10:38; 14:10-11; 17:21-23). Without this unity, God's plan of salvation could not have been completed. If Jesus was not God, His sacrifice could not atone for our sins. Being united with the Father also meant that the Son would do everything that was consistent with the Father's will. In the wilderness, Satan tempted Jesus to deny the Father, but He wouldn't. Because of Jesus' unity with the Father, the Son only did that which the Father willed.

Now with the imminent fulfillment of the Father's plan of salvation, these heavenly mysteries are being revealed. When we accept Christ into our hearts, we become united with God in a perfect union in the same way that the Son is united with the Father. This was done so that, through our witness, the Spirit might apply God's salvation to the hearts of sinners. Abiding in Christ is essential to performing our greater works. Paul writes, "To them God chose to make known how great among the Gentiles are the riches of the glory of this mystery, which is Christ in you, the hope of glory" (Col. 1:27). In order that we might do this greater work of presenting Christ to the world, God has given us "every spiritual blessing in the heavenly places in Christ" (Eph. 1:3). Abiding in Christ opens the way, so that the resources of heaven can flow into our mission. Once we commit to abiding in Christ, through obeying His commands, we can expect to accomplish greater works.

Jesus returned to the Father and sent the Spirit of Truth to us. And the Spirit testifies to Christ. *The Spirit is given so that we might know the mystery of the Trinity, that the Son is in the Father, and the Father is in the Son.* Jesus says that this truth cannot be understood without the Spirit. Our minds simply cannot comprehend the secret things of God. Now, not only do we understand the truth about God, we also know His will and involve ourselves in it. We commit to introducing others to Christ so that they too will be united to Him.

Our relationship with God is a powerful thing. As we obey God's commands, the Spirit's power flows through us. We become sensitive to the Spirit's leading and He uses us to open the eyes of those who are blind to the truth about Christ. Remember that God works through those who are living in obedience to the Word. Take time now to reflect on your union with Christ. Are there sins in your life that you need to confess, so that God's power will be in you to perform greater works?

Loving Obedience

Whoever has my commandments and keeps them, he it is who loves me. And he who loves me will be loved by my Father, and I will love him and manifest myself to him.

– JOHN 14:21

Read James 2:14-26

On the night of His arrest, Jesus taught His disciples the truth about God. He explained how the Father, Son, and Spirit work together to bring salvation to the world. The plan of God revealed the mystery of how the holy God was going to solve the problem of sin, so that unholy people could be accepted in His presence. The Father, Son, and Spirit revealed to us the depth of God's love. It must have been difficult for the disciples to grasp that Jesus is one with the Father. We can also struggle to understand this. However, when we do grasp the relationship of the Father and the Son, it transforms us. Knowing the truth about the Son compels us to take new and bold action.

Since the Son is one with the Father, then the Son must be obeyed just as the Father is to be obeyed. God established the Jewish nation as a testimony to the true God, Yahweh. They were to live in obedience to His commands. The first command was not to worship any other gods. God gathered the Jews at Mount Gerizim and Mount Ebal to recite the Law and pronounce curses on themselves if they were to disobey (Joshua 8:30-35). The Jews knew that obedience to God was required for His people, so that they would live long in the land that He was going to give them, thereby becoming a testimony to the nations. Unfortunately, the Jews failed to keep the commandments. Instead of loving God, they bowed down before idols, which means they loved other things more than God. Finally, God exiled them from the Promised Land that He had given to them.

Now, Jesus is reminding us of that commitment. The

New Covenant established through Jesus' death, and reaffirmed in the Lord's Supper, means that just as the Jews obeyed Yahweh, so too we who are in Christ need to obey Him. He is God and His commands should be of utmost importance to us. But having the commands of Christ is not enough. His followers must demonstrate their love for Christ by obeying them. *A follower of Christ doesn't just confess with his mouth that Jesus is Lord, but he also demonstrates that confession by obeying Christ.* We cannot proclaim that He is Lord without submitting to His Lordship over our lives.

Jesus tells us that He speaks the words of the Father, does the works of the Father, and reveals the Father. Jesus' words are authoritative. As the people of Israel were commanded to be holy because God was holy, so too we are to be holy by obeying Jesus' words. After His resurrection, Jesus commanded us to give testimony of His resurrection. We demonstrate our love for Christ when we tell others about the glory of the Son. As we do that, the Father reveals the Son to us. And, God uses our testimonies to bring others to faith, which gives us greater insight into the incredible work of Christ in redemption.

Many times, we are disappointed with ourselves for our lack of obedience. We follow the passions of our hearts and sin. But I have never met a Christian who regretted obeying Christ. When we obey and testify about Him to the world, we live in fellowship with Christ and grow in our love for Him. Do you regret not obeying God's commandments?

Revealing Christ To the World

*Judas (not Iscariot) said to him, "Lord, how is it that you will
manifest yourself to us, and not to the world?" Jesus answered him,
"If anyone loves me, he will keep my word, and my Father will love
him, and we will come to him and make our home with him.
Whoever does not love me does not keep my words. And the word
that you hear is not mine but the Father's who sent me."*

– JOHN 14:22-24

Read I Corinthians 3:16-23

Now that the mystery about the oneness of the Father
and Son was revealed, this mystery needed to be explained
to the world. Judas (not Iscariot) put forward an important
question: "If what you told us is so important then why are
you only sharing it with us? Everyone must hear of it." Judas
was correct. This was big news and needed to be told to the
entire world. But that was not Jesus' role. Jesus came to
fulfill the Father's plan of salvation. It was the Holy Spirit's
role to work through every believer to spread the news of
redemption throughout the world. Through the testimony
of believers, the world will know the true God.

*The church's mission is to know Christ and to make Him
known to all the world, so that His name will be glorified.* Jesus
explained how someone can know Him. It begins by loving
Christ. This means that we discard the idols in our lives and
only worship the true God. We can't love both God and the
world. For example, Jesus taught that we must choose
between our love for God and our love for money. Which
one have you chosen? If we have chosen Christ, we
demonstrate our choice by obeying His commands. It's our
obedience that honors God in front of non-believers. When
we obey Christ's commands, we experience the Father's
love, and as a result we grow closer to Him. It's the Holy
Spirit indwelling in us who helps us obey Christ's
commands and grow in knowledge of Him.

John has already told us that the Holy Spirit will fill us (v. 17). Now he writes that the Father and the Son will dwell in us. *God not only is involved in our salvation, but also in the daily lives of believers.* In the same way that God's glory filled the Holy of Holies in the Temple, so too God fills each believer. Our hearts are cleansed by the redemptive work of Christ on the cross, and He poured out His blood to make us holy before God. Now, God is near to us in a personal and intimate way. When we confess our sins, the obstacles that hinder our fellowship with God are removed.

Christ didn't reveal Himself to the world. Rather, He chose us to continue His work by sharing the Good News with the world. The Father, Son, and Spirit are in us for that purpose. Wherever we are, God's presence is with us. He is watching over us as we proclaim His greatness. The indwelling Christ works through our lives to bring others to the Risen Son of God. He gives us His words to speak so that even a heart of stone might respond to the gospel. But, Christ gives the world a choice: people can believe in Him, who is revealed through His church, or reject Him. Those who reject this message, reject God Himself. When people reject the gospel, they are declaring that they don't love Christ. By rejecting Christ, they are also rejecting the Father. The world has a choice, but it is our job to faithfully make Christ's salvation known to the world. How are you revealing the mystery of the oneness of the Father and the Son to the world?

Our Divine Teacher

These things I have spoken to you while I am still with you. But the Helper, the Holy Spirit, whom the Father will send in my name, he will teach you all things and bring to your remembrance all that I have said to you.

– JOHN 14:25-26

Read John 20:19-30

If you want to meet an important person, you need to make an appointment first. Otherwise they won't have time for you. But this is not the case with the most important person, Jesus. One thing that has always amazed me about Jesus is that no one ever needed an appointment to meet Him. They could come to Him in the middle of the night like Nicodemus or touch Him on the street like the woman with bleeding. We see this occurrence repeatedly in the gospels. So far in this dinner table conversation, Peter, Thomas, Philip, and Judas (not Iscariot) have asked questions, and Jesus patiently answered each of them. We, too, should never be afraid to come to Jesus with our questions. When we are confused, we can ask Him and He will answer us, just like He did with the disciples.

Once Jesus returns to heaven, He has promised to still be around through His Spirit to answer our questions. This is an important role of the Holy Spirit. Christ knows that we will continue to have many questions. It's normal to sometimes forget what was taught to us or to be confused by what we read in the Bible. But, God's Word is full of answers for us, and that's where the Holy Spirit comes in. He is our guide to help us understand the things of God. Whether we are in the village or the city, or whether we have much education or little, the Spirit is in us to answer the questions that arise in our hearts.

When you read the gospel stories, we are reading the very the words of Christ. We are taught directly by the Spirit just as if we were being taught by Jesus Himself. The Bible helps us understand more deeply who Christ is and the depth of His love for us. Even though we have read the stories of the Bible before, each time we read them the stories should speak to us again. This is evidence that the Spirit is indeed in you. Through the Word and His Spirit, God still speaks to us today revealing to us the spiritual truths about Jesus and His work of salvation.

Remembering, understanding, and obeying Christ's words is not possible without the Spirit. Neither can we do the works that Christ did without the Spirit. That is why Jesus told us that doing greater works is only possible, because He was going to the Father (John 14:12). Jesus' works demonstrated the power of God. We need the same power, for we can't do anything without the Holy Spirit. When Jesus went to the Father, the Spirit came upon us, and as a result, Jesus sent us forth to proclaim the gospel only after He gave us the Holy Spirit (John 20:21-23). Through the Spirit's power, we can do the works that Jesus did by sharing the Good News that people's sins can be forgiven in Christ. Whenever you go out, you can have complete confidence that God will give you everything you need as you testify for Him through the power of the Spirit. What are you asking to Holy Spirit to teach you today so that you are better equipped to testify to the world about Christ?

Filled with Peace

Peace I leave with you; my peace I give to you. Not as the world gives do I give to you. Let not your hearts be troubled, neither let them be afraid.

– JOHN 14:27

Read II Corinthians 11:23-33

What is the purpose of your life? It should be to be useful to the Kingdom of God. A faithful disciple doesn't love his life, but is instead willing to pay the cost of following Christ. You will only live for a short time on earth, but you will have all eternity in heaven. Being willing to die is different than wanting to die. No sane person wants to die. It's understandable to fear death. For many people, it's the fear of the process of dying that's most troubling, not what happens after death. Those are two completely different things. If I'm honest, I am quite angry with Adam. Why did he have to sin so that I am now under the penalty of death? I don't want to die. But if Adam could send a message to me, he would say: "If I had not eaten the fruit, you would have!" I want to live because God has created me for life. Sin has brought death and we are all under that penalty. If I must die, then let me die doing God's will and obeying His commands.

Paul boldly shared the gospel, often in the face of death. Because of his testimony, Paul received 40 lashes minus one. The instrument used to scourge Paul was made of leather and consisted of three strands. At the end of these strands was a small ball with spikes. With each lash, the balls would tear away Paul's skin. The scourging consisted of 13 lashes on the chest and 26 lashes on the back. Paul was scourged on five separate times (II Cor. 11:24). This meant 39 strikes times three strands, times five scourgings for a total of 585 wounds on Paul's body. You or I might have the courage to be scourged once for the gospel, because we haven't experienced how painful it is! But how many of us would be willing to be scourged a second time or even five times! We can feel so courageous, because we have not yet faced persecution. Amazingly, Paul didn't return home after being scourged. Rather, he continued his ministry, because he was filled with a sense of peace knowing that heaven was awaiting him when his job was done. He knew that the peace that Jesus gives doesn't depend on his situation, but on the promises of God and Jesus' presence with him.

Disciples cannot fulfill their calling if they consider their own well-being more important than the mission of God. Pride comes from the Devil. It destroys. When disciples focus on the worldly benefits and forget the spiritual blessings that God gives, they will no longer be faithful to the Lord's leading in their lives. A willingness to die or self-denial means that you are not focused on yourself, but that you seek first the Kingdom of God. God will provide everything else you need. If you want to be successful in ministry and become a faithful disciple, you must deny yourself every day. This may mean that you put to death all your future goals and ambitions to follow God. Although there may be many other ministry opportunities offered to you, you need to decide to stay in the place that God has prepared for you. God never leads you into a dead end. It's helpful to remember that your future isn't here on earth, but in the Father's house.

If you stop listening to Jesus' voice and start listening to the world or Satan, your heart will be filled with worry and fear in no time. Satan is not your friend; He wants to destroy your life. The world will tempt you to throw away your future, but you need to deafen your ears to those voices that don't come from God. Listen only to His Word, because it's the only voice that can be trusted. Jesus' peace comes from heaven, not from the world. The God who created you knows exactly what you need, so that you will be a good and faithful disciple. Are you at peace in your current situation?

The Joy of Obedience

You heard me say to you, "I am going away, and I will come to you."
If you loved me, you would have rejoiced, because I am going to the
Father, for the Father is greater than I. And now I have told you
before it takes place, so that when it does take place you may believe.

– JOHN 14:28-29

Read Philippians 2:6-11

If we're honest, we should admit that we look for situations that are advantageous to us. This is true even in picking a place of ministry. We think that we'll go wherever God calls us and do whatever He wills, but in reality, *we infuse God's call with our self-interest. It seems spiritual to say that God has given me a burden for a certain ministry when, in fact, it's our own desire that is leading us.* That is why surrendering yourself to God is so important. Many times, our desires get in the way of God doing greater works through us.

Jesus repeated to His disciples that He was going away, but that He would come back again for them. This is not what His disciples wanted to hear. Their self-interest told them to hold on to Jesus. They enjoyed His company, and they were greatly blessed to be a part of the amazing work that He was doing. Jesus' departure would be a great loss for them personally. But, there was to be no negotiating with Jesus. He was leaving because He was going to obey the will of the Father regardless of what was best for Himself. And He didn't obey begrudgingly, He did so with great joy.

We, too, should rejoice with Jesus, because His going away meant the Holy Spirit came. Now, we can do the greater works that Jesus wills for us to do. Jesus says we will rejoice, because we realize that the Father is greater than the Son. This doesn't mean that the Son is lesser than the Father. The Son is fully God and equal to the Father. Instead, we should understand this phrase as simply a statement that the Father has the commanding role in bringing salvation to the world. In John 10:29-30, Jesus says that the Father "is greater than all." Immediately following that statement, Jesus says, "I and the Father are one." Jesus is teaching us that it was the Father who planned salvation from before the world was created. That is why we view Him as primary or greater. The Son submitted to the will of the Father by fulfilling the Father's plan of salvation. This submission was an act of humility that lasted only for a time. Now the Son has returned to heaven and is worshipped with the Father as the Lord God Almighty.

There is a consequence that flows from the Father being primary. It means that we must be willing at every moment to surrender to His will. The Father is at work, through the Spirit, to bring the completed work of Christ to the world. He knows where workers are needed and sends them to these places. Even though it may seem that going there will lead to financial loss or greater family struggles, we are to rejoice because we have confidence in what the Father is doing. With all humility, we should accept the portion which God has prepared for us. Glorify His name by believing His promises for your spouse and children. No matter what happens, we can have complete confidence that the Father is directing our lives, and great joy can be found in submitting to His will. Nothing else will ever bring the true satisfaction that our souls are longing for. Are you content with the Father's will for your life?

Obeying the Father

I will no longer talk much with you, for the ruler of this world is coming. He has no claim on me, but I do as the Father has commanded me, so that the world may know that I love the Father. Rise, let us go from here.

– JOHN 14:30-31

Read Hebrews 4:14-5:10

Have you ever had a task to do that you didn't want to do? At times like this, we find so many excuses to avoid fulfilling our obligation. As Jesus faced His imminent death on the cross, He didn't delay for a moment; He continually moved forward with the Father's plan. Jesus was not teaching His disciples in the Upper Room as an excuse to delay this event. Instead, Jesus was explaining it to them so that, when it occurred, they would know for certain that this was God's plan and not the Devil's scheme. Now, the moment was at hand, the time for talking had ended. The time for the long-awaited sacrifice to be given for our atonement had arrived. Jesus certainly was different from other religious teachers. He was not interested in giving speeches of many words. His interest was only in obeying the Father, who willed for Jesus to die on the cross.

Jesus wants us to know clearly that His death was not a victory for the Devil. The "ruler of this world" tried to prevent Jesus from going to the cross. He tempted Jesus in the wilderness by offering all the kingdoms of the world to Him, if only Jesus would bow down and worship him. But Jesus refused. Satan also stirred up the hearts of the religious leaders on several occasions so that they would stone Jesus to death, but this wasn't God's plan. At the appointed time, Jesus was to die on the cross as a sacrifice for sins. Satan couldn't keep Jesus from fulfilling God's plan of salvation, no matter how hard he tried.

Jesus says that the Devil "has no claim over me." Satan

is the Accuser; He accuses us before God so that we will die and be punished. He has many claims over us, because he knows our sins. But Satan has no claim on Jesus, because He is different. Jesus lived a sinless life, which means Satan has nothing he can use to accuse Jesus before the Father (Heb. 4:15). That's why Jesus could be the perfect, unblemished Lamb that takes away the sins of the world. He didn't die for His own sin, but for the sin of all who believe in Him.

Jesus wants us to understand that Satan's power is limited. Jesus' death on the cross proves that Satan is under the control of God. In other words, Satan couldn't stop the Son from fulfilling the Father's plan. *Christ's death on the cross was not an act of subjugation, but a declaration to the world that the Father is on the throne in heaven.* Even Satan was being used to fulfill God's plan by inciting the people to hand Jesus over to the Romans to be crucified. The cross is Jesus' testimony of His great love for the Father. At Jesus' baptism, the Father declared His love for the Son, "This is my beloved Son, with whom I am well pleased" (Matt. 3:17). Now the Son declares His love for the Father by obeying the Father, even to the extent of dying on the cross (Isa. 53:10; Mark 10:45; II Cor. 5:21).

Jesus then asked His disciples to accompany Him. They left the dinner table, went through the dark streets of Jerusalem, and out of the city to the Garden of Gethsemane. The time approaching for the Son to be arrested and handed over for crucifixion. Jesus readily embraced this moment which would bring glory to the Father. Are you fully embracing God's calling on your life?

God Is at Work

I am the true vine, and my Father is the vinedresser.

– JOHN 15:1

Read Psalm 80:1-19

Throughout the Gospel of John, Jesus declares who He is saying: "I am...I am the Resurrection and the Life. I am the Good Shepherd." All of these declarations provide important insights into who Jesus is. He is God Incarnate, who is fulfilling the Father's plan of salvation. Moments before His arrest, Jesus once again teaches His disciples an important reality: "I am the True Vine." In the Upper Room, He taught His disciples that He is in the Father and the Father is in Him. And that He is also in His followers. This is a great statement. Jesus talks about the intimate union between the Father and the Son, as well as the fact that He will dwell within us (John 14:20). The disciples struggled on many occasions to understand Jesus' teaching. On this evening, they are once again struggling. After teaching about the truth of His relationship with the Father and our relationship to the Son, Jesus gives them an illustration that will open their minds to the important truth that He is teaching.

When Jesus says that He is the True Vine, He is not saying that there are false vines. Instead, He is differentiating between *true* and *shadow*. The Old Testament Temple worship, with its sacrifices, are pictures or shadows of the True Sacrifice that will be given to redeem us from our sins. This sacrifice was ultimately fulfilled in Christ, the Lamb of God, who takes away the sins of the world. The Old Testament portrays Israel as a vine (Ps. 80:8-16; Isa. 5:1-7). Israel is to be a people set aside by God to point the world towards the one true God and away from their idolatry. Because Israel sinned and worshipped false gods, the Father sent His Son as the True Vine to bring His salvation to the world. *Jesus is the True Vine. He alone is the fulfillment of God's plan to redeem the nations.* The vine exists to produce a harvest. Through the life-giving work of Jesus, a harvest will be reaped that will fill the storehouse of heaven with the souls of the redeemed.

And this harvest happens at the behest of the Father. For Jesus says, "The Father is the vinedresser." The vinedresser desires a harvest, so he plants and tends the vine. So too the Father has sent the Son and has worked to bring the Son to the cross. Through the sacrifice of the Son on the cross, the Father's work will achieve its goal. Throughout Jesus' life, the Father has watched over Him. No one could capture or harm Jesus before His time. Therefore, Jesus willingly submitted to the Father, the vinedresser. On several occasions, Jesus had the opportunity to avoid the cross, but He rejected Satan's attempts to derail the Father's plan (Matt. 4:1-11). In the Garden of Gethsemane, Jesus will wrestle in prayer but finally emerges victorious saying, "Not as I will, but as you will" (Matt. 26:39). The Son submitted to the Father, just as a vine submits to the vinedresser.

The Father, as vinedresser, shows how active He is in our salvation. A vinedresser plants a vine and nurtures it with the expectation that it will bear fruit. Planting a vine is costly, but it's the only way to gather a harvest. The Father has invested much; therefore, He is actively making sure the harvest is produced. Since before the creation of the world, the Father has been at work to produce a harvest through the Son. And even now, the Father is still at work so that we produce fruit for the glory of His name. How are you seeing the Father working to produce a harvest?

Dead Branches

Every branch in me that does not bear fruit he takes away...

– JOHN 15:2a

Read Mark 11:12-23

When I moved into a house that I recently rented, there was a mango tree in the backyard. Unfortunately, the owner informed me that the tree had never born fruit. I shared that information with the man who was cutting my grass. He told me, "I can make it so the tree bears fruit next year." And because I love to eat mangos, I enthusiastically told him to do whatever he thought was necessary. It wasn't long until I heard the cutting of branches as there were lopped off the tree. Later that afternoon, I went outside to see what he did. What I saw shocked me. The tree, which was previously lush and provided shade to the house, was now barren. Incredible. He cut most the branches off. There was little left apart from the tree trunk. Although I wanted to be angry, I kept my emotions under control. And you know what? The following year there were many mangos growing on that tree. This gardener knew how to prune a tree so that it would bear much fruit.

Our Heavenly Father knows even more about how to prune, so that much fruit grows in our lives. *He knows what must be stripped away so our lives will bear the fruit that He desires.* The Father sees every branch—each of us—and works in our lives so that His purpose is accomplished. But, the pruning process can be painful. It may mean standing in front of others to confess your sins, or being willing to give up something that's your right to have. Or you may need to bear the wrongs of others. If we're willing, the pruning process will go forward. It's my desire to not only bear fruit, but *much* fruit.

Remember, the Lord desires fruit and not just leaves. It's easy to be impressed by branches full of large green leaves, but God sees it differently. Don't be deceived by hypocrites that seem so spiritual yet in the end are not only not pruned, but are severed from the vine altogether. The leaves of religious works can quickly lead to pride. When you examine your life, don't be impressed by *external*, religious evidences that are not reflective of an *internal*, spiritual reality. Even if their lives seem to be blessed by God, don't be deceived. Not all blessings are from God. In the Kingdom of God, branches with lots of leaves are often cut off, and branches that don't appear so lush, are the ones that often produce the most fruit.

In the same way that the Son humbled Himself to the Father, so we too must humble ourselves so that we bear more fruit. Denying ourselves means sacrificing our leaves so that God's purpose is achieved—to bear much fruit. Many who are proud may continue to nurture their leaves, because they know that if their leaves fall away, their true selves will be evident to all: that, in reality, they aren't bearing any fruit. Those who abide in Christ are not afraid to be seen as lowly (without leaves), because they want the fruit to be seen and thereby bring glory to Christ. May the Lord prune all the leaves in your life, so you know that you have true faith.

If we want to bear fruit, we must abide in the vine. Sometimes we think when we proclaim the gospel to someone and invite them to receive Christ, we have done enough. We think that we have brought another soul into the kingdom. But Jesus teaches us that we have only just begun the work. It's His desire that *every* believer continually abides in the vine. It's not enough for sinners to only pray to receive Christ. They must bear fruit. Those who don't bear fruit are not in Christ. Faith is more than a verbal confession. Remember, *external* confessions can't save you; there must be an *internal* reality that is reflected by that confession—a changed life! Are you bearing fruit?

Pruned Branches

...and every branch that does bear fruit he prunes...

– JOHN 15:2b

Read Philippians 2:12-18

Every branch receives attention from the Father, the vinedresser. When the machete is swung at the branch, certainly pain will be experienced. Some branches will be completely cut off and thrown away, because they have rejected Christ. Others will be pruned, because they have faith in Christ. Being pruned by the Father means experiencing some pain in order to grow. If we truly want more fruit in our lives, then we must surrender ourselves to the Father. Blessed are the believers who understand that the Father wants to prune their lives, so they can grow more into His likeness. By submitting to Him through this process, His work will be made perfect in your life. To bear much fruit, you must be willing to be pruned. There's no other way. Your heart and your character must constantly be examined by the Word of God.

Something in my life that was not pleasing to God was my rebellious spirit. In college, God used several of my friends to expose that sin so it could be pruned from my life. We were serving the Lord together in Argentina. Our group went from town to town showing the Jesus Film in the town square. One afternoon, we were raising up the large screen for that evening's showing. I climbed up the pole and unfurled the screen. Those on the ground said that the screen was high enough. Nevertheless, I continued to climb, because I wanted to raise the screen up even higher. After the movie started, my three friends called me aside. We sat in a quiet place so we could talk. They asked, "Why do you like to rebel?" Immediately, I defended myself saying: "I am not rebellious." My answer alone was enough to prove their point. I realized that I was indeed rebellious. The Lord made me recognize that I always thought I was the right one, and everyone else was wrong. Consequently, I wouldn't follow instructions from others. That night, God began changing me. While I still have a tendency to rebel, praise God that I continue to be pruned by the Father.

It's all about the fruit. That's why our character needs to be continually pruned, so we will bear more fruit. This is a discipleship principle: *A disciple continues to grow every day through the confession of sins.* Jesus told Peter that he needed to be washed (John 13:10). Our sins need to be washed through confession, because they can prevent us from bearing fruit. Confession of sins is evidence that we are in Christ, because we are experiencing the active pruning process by our Father. Our failings teach us humility, so that we no longer feel as though we need to defend ourselves whenever the Spirit convicts us of sin in our lives. "The steadfast love of the Lord never ceases; his mercies never come to an end; they are new every morning; great is your faithfulness" (Lam. 3:22-23). Those who confess their sins will receive comfort.

Many people serve the Lord, because they want to be acknowledged by others. They want others to see how successful they are so they receive the praise of men. But this originates from an ungodly motive, because true fruit glorifies the Father, not us. Jesus taught, "Let your light shine before others, so that they may see your good works and give glory to your Father who is in heaven" (Matt. 5:16). The leaves of our lives steal the glory due to God, because it puts the spotlight on us. Ask the Lord today to reveal the sin hiding in your heart. Don't delay in confessing that sin to God. If you need to be reconciled with another, do so immediately. Remember, God's mercy is new every morning. What needs to be pruned from your life so that you can bear fruit? Pride? Anger? Laziness?

Very Fruitful Branches

...that it may bear more fruit.

– JOHN 15:2c

Read Matthew 25:14-30

In John 15:2, we see a progression taking place from those who don't bear fruit, to those who do bear fruit, and finally to those who bear *much* fruit. This verse teaches an important principle. *Since Christ is working in us so that we bear much fruit, we should not be satisfied with only* some *fruit.* Christ desires that we continue to grow and bear fruit to become more like Him. Satisfaction with what we have done can threaten our faith and growth. In the Book of Judges, the people of Dan wanted to attack the city of Laish. After scouting out the city, they discovered that the city was filled with "a people quiet and unsuspecting" (Judges 18:27). Because the people of Laish were satisfied with themselves, they let their guards down and they were easily defeated by the people of Dan.

Those who become satisfied and comfortable in their spiritual lives no longer have a desire to strive for more. They see fruit in their lives and think that they have done enough, especially compared to others. A true disciple is never satisfied with only a little bit of fruit. They want more than just some fruit. They desire to do even greater works for God's glory. In the Parable of the Talents, the men received differing amounts of talents. These men were expected to be good stewards and make the talents earn more talents. The one who received five talents was not satisfied with only earning an additional four talents. He could have compared himself to the one who received two talents, and earned an additional two talents, and thought that he was the most productive. However, the goal is not to do more than those around us, but to produce fruit according to God's will for us. We must be accountable for every talent that is entrusted to us.

I praise God that He has entrusted to me a ministry in which I must work hard. If I weren't in a ministry like this, I wouldn't have grown into the man that I am today. Because I am serving in a difficult field, it forces me to have greater faith and trust in Christ. Every day I face those who oppose the gospel. If I had been in a comfortable ministry all these years, I wouldn't have grown as much as I have. Some people in ministry limit themselves to what they will teach on or do. They learn only a few things and routinely do those things. They serve, but not with a sense of urgency. Since I work with those who oppose the gospel, I am forced to pray more diligently. And, I know that I can only do what I do with the Spirit's help. You, too, should rejoice if you find yourself in a ministry that is challenging. Perhaps, you are struggling to meet your family's needs with the funds that you receive each month, or you are constantly harassed by the authorities. You can rejoice, because these hardships can drive you to a deeper abiding relationship with Christ.

The vinedresser looks at the branch with the purpose in mind to make each branch even more fruitful. You can rejoice because God Himself is involved in this process. We know that our struggle is not in vain, because God's power is at work within us. It's the very life of Christ flowing through us, so that our striving produces even more fruit for His glory. Blessed are those who are persecuted because of the gospel, and blessed are those who struggle to make ends meet, so that they will learn to have complete faith and dependence on Christ. In this way, the power of Christ is made evident in our lives. The Father cares about every branch and its fruit, and He is personally overseeing the entire pruning process. You can have confidence that the Father is at work in you. What additional fruit is God wanting you to produce?

Made Holy by Christ

Already you are clean because of the word that I have spoken to you.

— JOHN 15:3

Read I John 3:1-10

Many Christians are filled with doubts. These doubts come from Satan who fills our minds with lies. The Apostle Peter describes Satan as our adversary (I Pet. 5:8). *Satan is opposed to Christ and is working diligently to destroy our faith and render us fruitless in our Christian lives.* Throughout the day, Satan is tempting us to sin. He puts thoughts in our minds, so that we will disobey God, and lies to us saying that there will be no consequences for our sin. This is exactly what Satan did with Adam and Eve when he told them, "You will not surely die" (Gen. 3:4). Similarly, we are tempted to sin and often succumb to disobeying God. Immediately after we fall, Satan is right there accusing us with more lies. He tries to make us think that God will never forgive us. Truly Satan is our conniving adversary.

Jesus had just told His disciples that there are branches that are to be cut off and branches that are to be pruned. After we sin, Satan fills our minds with thoughts that maybe we are a branch to be cut off. He is the one who fills our minds with doubts, which is one of the consequences of our sin. How do we know if we are a branch that will be cut off or only pruned? Jesus' words give us confidence. Jesus has told us that He will never leave us, and that He is going to the Father to prepare a place for us. Those who have believed in Christ will *not* be cut off. *Our salvation is not dependent on our works, but on Christ's work.* No matter how many sins we commit and how terrible those sins are, Jesus has paid our debt in full. Jesus says that we have already been cleaned. This is a cleaning unlike anything that the world or other religions can offer. Often, when a person sins, they try to restore themselves before God through prayer, fasting, etc. But none of our works can ever remove the debt of sin before God. This is another one of Satan's deceptions. He tells us that if we work hard enough, we can pay our debt of sin. However, each day, we know that our debt increases because we cannot perfectly obey God's law. Only Christ has done that. Therefore, only Christ can pay our debts, because He didn't have to pay for any debts of His own. Jesus reminds us now that we are already cleaned. No more doubts. It's done. We can have complete certainty in our salvation.

One of the ways we become clean is through Christ's Word. It is the *true* revelation of God. Everything that Jesus spoke points us to the Father. For Jesus is the Way, the Truth, and the Life (John 14:6). Listening to His Word and obeying it is the key. His Word gives us the power to put away Satan's deceptions. Satan is a liar, but Jesus' Words are true. Jesus tells us that if we believe in Him we will have eternal life, so we don't have to rely on our own works and righteousness. We don't enter Paradise through being good. It's our sins that have disqualified us from Paradise, because nothing unclean can be in Paradise. God's Word tells us that there is no way to the Father apart through Jesus. When we accept Jesus into our hearts and confess Him as Lord with our mouths, we will be cleaned (Rom. 10:9). And no one can cut us off from the vine—ever.

Although we have been cleaned, we still need to be pruned; so fill your mind with God's Word, and close your ears to the accuser. Romans 12:1 tells us "to be transformed by the renewal of your mind." Only then will our doubts go away as we live righteous lives according to God's Word. What lies of Satan have you been listen to and what truth do you find in Jesus?

Quality Fruit

Abide in me, and I in you. As the branch cannot bear fruit by itself,
unless it abides in the vine, neither can you, unless you abide in me.

– JOHN 15:4

Read Luke 3:1-9

Abide. Abide. Abide. Jesus repeatedly draws our attention to this principle in our spiritual lives. The purpose of our lives is to glorify God by bearing fruit as we do the works that Jesus did. And Jesus desires that every disciple bears fruit. *God is glorified when we live holy lives, obey His commands and give witness to the resurrection of Christ.* It's only possible to accomplish this goal through abiding in Christ. Only then does the power and life of Christ flow through us producing the kind of fruit that makes a lasting difference. A branch cannot produce fruit by itself. Without the life of the vine within it, the branch will just shrivel up and die.

If you aren't bearing fruit, you are not fulfilling God's purpose for your life. On one occasion when Jesus was going to the Temple, He passed by a fig tree with many leaves. Jesus was hungry and wanted to eat the fruit from that tree, but there was none. There were only leaves, so He cursed the tree. The disciples were taken aback. This healthy, lush tree withered and died because of that curse. This event highlights the relevant principle for us—Jesus desires that we bear fruit. If we are not producing fruit, then we are in danger of being cut off and thrown away. That fig tree was symbolic of the nation of Israel. They were full of beautiful leaves such as the Temple, the Law of Moses, and the history of God's miraculous work on their behalf, but they didn't abide in God, so they produced no fruit. They should have embraced Jesus as the promised Messiah, but instead they crucified Him.

We face a similar danger. *If we say that we believe in Christ, but we are not producing fruit from that relationship, we are only*

97

deceiving ourselves. Many people serving God seem so spiritual but, in reality, they are not producing fruit. Jesus desires the fruit that only comes from a relationship with Him; not the fruit of people who are spiritual showoffs. Some churches rent nice places so many people will attend their services. They believe if a lot of people come, certainly that indicates that God is there. They appear prosperous and beautiful from the outside, but if you look behind the leaves on these churches, there is no certainty that you would find fruit that lasts. Oftentimes, churches are afraid of proclaiming the whole message of the Bible, because if the rich people in attendance are put off, they will take their offering and move to another church. Branches don't bear fruit because they are supported by the offering of wealthy people. Branches bear fruit because they are abiding in Christ alone.

Don't be discouraged if there are not a lot of people following your ministry. God only asks you to keep serving faithfully, proclaiming the whole message of the Bible. Remember, Jesus' ministry went from 5,000 followers in John 6 down to 12 disciples, and one of them betrayed Him. If this happened in our churches today, we would accuse the leadership of not praying enough or living in sin. But Jesus was not interested in a ministry full of leaves. The Lord said that fruit is more important than leaves. So often, because we want to be seen as successful, we try to get as many followers as possible. Somehow, we think that others will notice how awesome we are.

But Jesus' standard of success is not the *quantity* of leaves, but *quality* fruit. The leaves of success and external religiosity can encumber you from abiding in Christ. They need to be pruned away. We must be willing to leave the external standards of success, because they can hinder the producing of fruit. God intentionally prunes away these things from our lives, so that we no longer pursue the acknowledgement of others, but produce the fruit that He desires instead. God doesn't want leaves, He wants fruit. How are you defining success?

Getting the Relationship Right

I am the vine; you are the branches.

– JOHN 15:5a

Read II Corinthians 1:3-11

The fruit produced by the branch is the same kind as the vine. It would be really weird if the branches of a grape vine produced oranges. The more we abide in Christ, the more we produce the fruit of Christ and will look like Christ. If we are continually abiding in Him, then what we desire will be the same as what Christ desires. The branches abiding in the vine cannot do anything on their own. Think of what would happen if the branch said, "I don't want to remain in this vine anymore. I don't want to produce grapes. I want to grow oranges." Once the branch stopped being in the vine, it would not produce oranges, but would immediately die. Abiding in the vine means producing the fruit of the vine.

But so often we do something similar to this by trying to dictate to God what we will do. We tell the Lord, "This is *my* dream. This is what *I* want to do with my life," even though God has a completely different plan for us. In order to submit to God's plan for our lives, we must first deny ourselves and the desires of our heart. God isn't happy with just any type of fruit. *The fruit that pleases the heart of God is the fruit that reflects the character and work of Christ.* For this to happen, we must deny ourselves in the same way that Jesus denied Himself. Instead of pursuing earthly status and comfort, we seek first the kingdom of God. And in doing so, the Father is glorified.

It's interesting to note the type of fruit Jesus chooses in this parable. Of all the plants that produce fruit, Jesus chose the grape vine to describe our relationship with Him. Why didn't Jesus say, "I am the jackfruit tree"? Why did He say, "I am the grape vine"? You would have thought that Jesus would have picked a strong and mighty tree. I can't think of a more interesting tree in the entire world than the jackfruit tree even though it produces one of the ugliest-looking fruits imaginable. Instead of being smooth, the fruit is lumpy with strange nodes on the skin. However, the fruit tastes delicious. Each fruit can weigh up to 35 kilograms. This means that that branches on the jackfruit tree must be able to support a very heavy weight. If the branches are not strong, they will bend to the earth as the fruit grows and eventually break off.

Yet, Christ didn't describe our relationship with Him with a picture of a jackfruit tree. He, instead, chose the grape vine. Even without fruit, the grape vine's branches are so weak that they must be tied up to wire so they won't fall to the ground. These branches have no strength in and of themselves to support their own weight. And this is without the added weight of the leaves and fruit. *Jesus is giving us a realistic picture of our ourselves. We are incapable of producing spiritual fruit in and of ourselves.* We don't have the strength to win in this spiritual battle. And even when we try to serve in our own strength, Satan opposes us with his much greater strength. Therefore, if we don't constantly abide in Christ and draw our strength from Him, we will not bear fruit.

The secret to bearing much fruit is abiding in the vine and being fully aware that we are weak and incapable of producing fruit on our own. You and I are not so special that we can do something for God in our own strength. Abiding in Christ is all about depending completely on Christ in every area of your life. If we try to bear fruit in our own strength, we will certainly fail. Fruit that lasts is only the result of the life of Christ working through us. That's why Jesus said, "*I* am the vine." Whose strength are you serving in? Your strength or Christ's strength?

Only One Vine

Whoever abides in me and I in him, he it is that bears much fruit,
for apart from me you can do nothing.

– JOHN 15:5b

Read Matthew 6:19-34

Jesus' statement seems to be contrary to our experience. Apart from Christ, you can do many things. The world is full of people producing many good things. Libraries are full of books recording the theories of great thinkers. Our lives are more comfortable, because of the technological progress made by creative people. Yet, when they die, they will be surprised to discover that what they produced here on earth cannot be brought to heaven. The fruit that Jesus is referring to is the fruit that God desires. Jesus teaches us that apart from Him we can do none of the work that He desires for us to do. We can't bring new believers to the throne of God. Only God can do that, so we must abide in Christ.

Every day you have a choice to make—will you live for Christ or for something else? Sprinkled throughout the pages of Scripture are people faced with that same choice. For example, the people of Israel had to choose whether they would worship the one true God or idols. Jesus gave the Jews a choice of worshiping Him as the Messiah or to follow their traditions. Over and over again, people were asked to choose. This was not a one-time choice, but a daily choice that they needed to make. All that you will do will be impacted by that choice. You will either do things for Christ's glory or for your own.

Every day, I need to remind myself that I am only a servant and not a master. I have always been impressed when the Apostle Paul says that he is the *least* of all the apostles. And on another occasion, he said that he was the *chief* of sinners. Despite his calling as an Apostle, Paul never forgot who he was. Many of us easily forget who we are once we are given a leadership position. We think we've arrived, losing sight of our true identity. And, if we're not careful, we can feel entitled to receive the benefits of our position. But a servant lets God decide what benefits they will be given, and lets God choose where they will serve. Our earthly comforts are not what is important. Being in the place that God has prepared for us is. *Why?* Because all of us must abide in Christ.

If you are abiding in Christ, you are continually seeking His will for your life. There can only be one vine. This may seem obvious, but it's hard to implement. It can be outright painful, because all other vines sprouting in our lives must be removed, so that only the true vine remains. It requires regular self-examination to see what possible sprouts are growing that would threaten to replace Christ. And, whenever these sprouts appear, immediately uproot them and throw them away before they get too big, because the bigger they are, the more painful they are to remove. Has your family become a sprout that is replacing Christ as your vine? If someone is proposing a marriage that will take you away from your calling, obey your calling. Many women in ministry are single not because they are undesirable, but because they choose to be faithful to their callings rather than getting married. Don't replace obedience to God with a marriage that may not give you what you are looking for or, more importantly, be God's will for your life. The love of money can also threaten to consume your heart. It's the root of all evil. Don't destroy the future of your ministry, because you didn't trust God to provide for your needs. He has a plan for your life.

Peter wrote, "in your hearts honor Christ the Lord as holy," (I Pet. 3:15). Honoring Christ means to set Him apart by uprooting all the other sprouts wanting to push Him aside. Start today. If the vines that are sprouting in your heart are not removed, they will keep you from abiding in Christ. What sprouting vines do you need to remove?

False Faith

If anyone does not abide in me he is thrown away like a branch and withers; and the branches are gathered, thrown into the fire, and burned.

– JOHN 15:6

Read Matthew 23:23-36; Galatians 6:7

True faith is known by its fruit. *False faith doesn't produce fruit. It doesn't accept the Father's means of salvation, and it doesn't involve itself in doing the works that Jesus did.* These branches are thrown into the fire because they are dead and fruitless. Branches that seem to give a semblance of life because there are many leaves, are only a deception. Some who claim to worship God can seem spiritual, but they have not yet received the grace of God. Israel is an example of that. Israel was given Moses and the Temple as a testimony to the gospel that the Lamb of God would come to take away the sins of the world. Instead of abiding in God, they rejected God's grace and manipulated the Law and the Temple to justify their wicked hearts. And because Israel rejected Jesus the Messiah, Israel was rejected by God.

Judas is another example of false faith. He was a branch that was *externally* connected to the true vine, but *internally* he was abiding in a completely different vine. For three years, Judas followed Christ. He was sent to villages in Israel to proclaim the Kingdom of God and to cast out demons. Looking from the outside, it seems that Judas was successful in ministry. He also witnessed miracles and heard the teachings of Jesus firsthand. Judas enjoyed many of the blessings that we all long to enjoy. However, when things were not going according to Judas' plans, the true love of His heart became apparent to all. This love was money. He had the external forms of a disciple, but his heart never really was filled with love for Christ. Don't be deceived. *Many will appear to be holy, diligent in prayer, and willing to serve, but they are not abiding in Christ.*

Some believers wear spiritual clothes, but have the heart of Judas. As long as the situation in their ministry is to their benefit, they smile broadly and praise the Lord. But when the situation turns on them, they immediately complain and threaten others in the ministry. I have often witnessed disciples threatening other disciples. And on several occasions, I have been threatened as well. We each need to evaluate our hearts. Perhaps externally you are covered with leaves, but your heart is withered. Growing in Christ means that we will produce the fruit of becoming like Christ (II Cor. 3:18). Not only will our character become like Christ, but we will also produce physical fruit of souls being brought to faith in Christ and good works reflecting Christ's love to the world.

In the end, the branches that are only externally connected to the vine, but don't have the life of the vine flowing through them, will be cut off and burned. These branches will be destroyed and will not be given another chance. Grape branches are useless except for bearing fruit. If I cut down a coconut tree because it doesn't produce coconuts, I could still use the wood from that tree to build a house. However, grape branches have no other use, so they are destroyed. These branches were not even used to cook food since they burned so rapidly. It's the same way with our lives. Outside of Christ, there is nothing in our lives that can be used to build God's Kingdom. On the Day of Judgment, all those who have false faith will be thrown into the fire of Hell. When that happens, many will defend themselves saying that they ministered in Christ's name, but Jesus will say that He never knew them. If today you realize that you have a heart like Judas, a heart that loves something other than Christ, don't reject the grace of God. Repent by confessing you know that your religious works can't get you to heaven, and accept the grace of God so that you can abide in the vine. Then the life of Christ will flow through you. Are you abiding in Christ?

Powerful Prayers

If you abide in me, and my words abide in you, ask whatever you wish, and it will be done for you.

– JOHN 15:7

Read I John 3:19-24

Jesus gives us an incredible promise: If we abide in Him, we will bear much fruit and can ask anything in His name, and He will do it for us—anything in His name. Wow, that is awesome. But did Jesus really mean that the Father would immediately give us whatever we ask for? No, He didn't. The key to understanding this truth is found in the first part of the verse: "If you abide in me, and my words abide in you." Prayer is not something that is automatically answered by God as though God is a robot. *Prayer is answered because we are in Christ, and He works through His children who are one in heart with His mission.*

Being "in Christ" is so crucial that the phrase is used 175 times in the New Testament. Clearly, no fruit will be produced in our lives apart from being in Christ. We can pray and continually ask God for fruit, but God will not give us fruit because fruit only grows as a result of the life of Christ flowing through us. But for those in Christ, even while experiencing great difficulties, we are promised that we will have great joy in the end because we bore fruit.

In the same way that a husband and wife enjoy an intimate relationship with one another so that they can understand each other, so too do we, who are abiding in Christ, better understand God's will and heart's desire. The more we study and meditate on His Word, the more we will understand Jesus' desire that the Father is glorified (Phil. 2:11) through the salvation of sinners (I Tim. 2:4-5). Those who understand God's desire will actively pray for His will to be done. Our prayers should center around the subject of proclaiming the gospel to the whole world. God wants all of us to take part in His mission through prayer. What an incredible opportunity we have to proclaim the gospel to the ends of the earth. *Through our evangelism and prayer, we become co-workers with Christ.* When we share the gospel with someone, we are also praying that the Holy Spirit will work in their heart and bring them to saving faith.

Jesus has already instructed us on how to prevent egotistical prayers that are not in accordance with His will. He said that branches that are abiding in Him will be pruned. In order to grow spiritually, Jesus will be continually pruning us. Through that pruning process, our desires and ambitions will be purified by the Lord so they are in accordance with His plan for the world. Then as we make our requests to God, our prayers will be in line with God's will. If you were to plant some rice, would you expect mangos to grow from those plants? Of course not. Fruit can only be produced by the same kind of plant. That's Jesus' point.

It's also important to note that Jesus changed the metaphor. Previously, Jesus said that *He* will abide in us. Now, Jesus says that *His words* will abide in us. Both of these statements mean the same thing. Jesus is the Word of God made flesh; He is the true revelation of the Father to the world. Jesus and His Word cannot be separated. The eternal Word of God resided in the physical body of Jesus Christ. So, as we meditate on the Word of God, the Holy Spirit leads us into understanding God's will. As a result, we deny ourselves and submit to His will so that His plans may be accomplished through us. If you are already praying, reading God's Word, and submitting to Him, then ask God to give you greater boldness to pray in accordance with His will. The Father's name will be glorified to the ends of the earth through your prayers. What are you praying for?

Fruit That Glorifies God

*By this my Father is glorified, that you bear much fruit and so prove
to be my disciples.*

– JOHN 15:8

Read Ephesians 2:1-10

Jesus reveals the Father's will to us, because He wants
us to bear much fruit. Jesus has already told us, "Truly, truly,
I say to you, whoever believes in me will also do the works
that I do; and greater works than these will he do, because I
am going to the Father" (John 14:12). Jesus fulfilled the
Father's plan of salvation. Now the Father wants to fill
heaven with the souls of people redeemed through Jesus'
sacrifice. God does not want only a few people to be saved;
He wants all people to be saved for His glory because of His
great love for us.

Too many disciples are satisfied with too little results.
Of course, we should praise God for the one to two people
who believe through our ministry. But every day hundreds
of thousands of people are born throughout the world. And
the majority of those babies are born to non-believing
families. It's staggering to contemplate that the non-
Christian population is growing larger every year. If we
honestly evaluate ourselves, we should rejoice with those we
have already won for Christ, but should be dissatisfied
because there are so many more people that still need to be
reached with the gospel. *Those who are wise will understand that
the gospel must be proclaimed widely and quickly, so that the ripe
harvest will be immediately brought into God's kingdom.*

God is glorified with every sinner that repents. We're
told in Scripture, that the angels in heaven rejoice whenever
the lost is found (Luke 15:10). God wants to harvest the
fruit of repentance from every tribe, language, people, and
nation. Nobody will be rejected because of their economic
status, education, or place of birth. All of us have the same
standing before God. All of us are sinners saved by grace,

and not by works. God is glorified when sinners repent, because that repentance is the fruit or evidence of God's mercy and greatness. Only He is capable of paying our debt of sin and bringing us to heaven. Praise His name now and forever and ever!

The presence of fruit gives praise to the vinedresser, and branches that bear fruit are performing the function they were created for. That's why they don't need to be praised. Too often we put the spotlight on the fruit at the end of the branch by exclaiming, "Wow, that fruit sure makes the branch look beautiful." It's so easy then for the branch to steal the glory for itself. Remember, Jesus said: "Apart from me you can do nothing." The presence of fruit gives glory to the vine and the vinedresser, but the branches that are glorified grow bigger and bigger until no other branches can grow on the vine. When we feel like we have done great things for God and steal His praise for ourselves, we are actually killing off the ministry of others and opposing God. Remember, every branch can be cut off, but the vine will continue to live. But if the vine is removed, none of the branches can bear fruit any longer and will immediately die.

The fruit of the gospel growing in our lives is evidence that we are Jesus' disciples. Disciples understand their Master's teachings and apply them to their lives. In Ephesians 2:10, it says that we are God's creation made to do the good works that the Father has prepared for us beforehand. This means that before everything was made by God, He created and appointed us to produce fruit for His glory. Disciples understand that they are not presenting their own deeds to God. The only reason they are bearing fruit at all is because of Christ working through them. When disciples comprehend God's desire that all might be saved, they will understand that abiding in Christ through His word and prayer is the only way more fruit will be produced. Do you understand God's will for you?

Confident in God's Love

As the Father has loved me, so have I loved you. Abide in my love.

— JOHN 15:9

Read Matthew 3:13-17; 17:1-5

At the start of Jesus' earthly ministry, He came to the Jordan River where John was baptizing new believers. Jesus told John to baptize Him for He is the Lamb of God, who would take away the sins of the world. Jesus' baptism was actually the start of His journey to Calvary, where He would die as a sacrifice for our sins. Immediately after Jesus was baptized, the Father spoke from heaven saying: "This is my beloved Son, with whom I am well pleased." The Father confessed His love and pleasure for the Son. There was another time when the gospel records the Father speaking from heaven. It was when Jesus was on His way to Jerusalem, where He would be crucified. Jesus went up on a mountain and was transfigured sharing His Father's glory. Moses and Elijah appeared with Jesus, too. They discussed "his departure (exodus), which he was about to accomplish in Jerusalem" (Luke 9:31). Again, the Father spoke from heaven saying that Jesus was His beloved Son.

Both at the baptism and transfiguration, we were told about the Father's love for the Son. Jesus fulfilled the Father's will by becoming our sacrifice. He was willing to empty Himself for us, taking the form of a lowly servant. Because Jesus knew how great His Father's love was for Him, He was willing to do this. Finally, when Jesus breathed His last breath on the cross, He cried out: "Father, into your hands I commit my spirit" (Luke 23:46). Jesus was willing to die because He had complete confidence in the Father's love for Him. That love gave Him the boldness to fulfill the Father's plan of salvation. The perfect eternal love of the Father for the Son was crucial to bringing salvation to mankind, because God loves the world. It's His desire that no one should perish; He wants all to be saved. In spite of their rebellion against Him, people are valuable to God. We deserved punishment and death for our sins, but the Father's great love for us brought us life instead through the sacrifice of the Son.

This same love is now available to us. It's not limited only to the Father and the Son. The Son faced death on the cross with confidence, only because He knew the perfect love of the Father. The love which brought the fulfillment of the Father's plan of salvation is now given to us through Christ, so that we might bring this salvation to the world—our mission. Undoubtedly, we will face many hardships as we do this. In fact, we might quite possibly be misunderstood, arrested, persecuted, and even killed. Yet, it is the love of Christ—the same love that exists between the Father and Son—that compels us to do it. When we risk our lives and are willing to die for Christ, we do so knowing that our spirit has been committed into the hands of our Great High Priest. *It is God's love for us that motivates us to do greater works, because we know that whatever price we pay, nothing can separate us from the love of Christ (Rom. 8:38-39).*

Abiding in Christ's love is crucial for us to do His work and be right with God. But oftentimes, if we're not careful, our sin can replace our love for Christ with our own self-love. When this happens, our priorities are no longer Christ's priorities, but our own. This shift keeps us from living for God's glory. As Christ's disciples, it's important to remember that dying to self is possible only by abiding in Christ. We can face any situation because of our security in Christ. How are you abiding in His love?

Living in Grace

If you keep my commandments, you will abide in my love, just as I have kept my Father's commandments and abide in his love.

– JOHN 15:10

Read Hebrews 5:7-9

Satan is actively working to keep us from abiding in Christ so that God's mission will not be accomplished through us. Satan tells us that it is normal to sin or not obey God's commands. After all, not even Adam and Eve could keep God's command. Satan downplays the seriousness of sin as well as its consequences. We must recognize the Devil and his work. He is both a liar and an accuser. Since the beginning, Satan has been deceiving believers so they do not obey God and then accusing them after they sin saying that God will never forgive them. The Devil's schemes are evil.

Some churches have scarred disciples by emphasizing obedience to the commands of God rather than focusing on living in grace. Teachers tell their disciples that they must obey God's commands or else God will punish them. These disciples in turn agonize over the sins they commit. For instance, Jesus told us that when you lust in your heart, you have already committed adultery. In today's world where we are bombarded by sexual images, it is a real struggle to keep our hearts pure and free from lust. We find ourselves again breaking the commandments and are consumed by guilt. And Satan is right there accusing us saying that God will not forgive you this time. He will cut off the His relationship with you. Therefore, we beat ourselves up over how we have once again failed God.

Yet our experience with God is not to be like this. After we put our faith in Christ, we live or abide in His love. We have a relationship with Him that can never be broken by anything that we do. We are eternally secure in our salvation because Jesus has paid it all. The guilt we experience when we sin is because we are sensitive to God and desire to do His will. We understand His grace and our status as a child of God so we respond differently to our guilt. We run to the cross because Jesus has paid our debt of sin in full. Satan no longer has a basis to accuse us before God. *And when we confess our sin, the work of Christ becomes greater in our life as we understand how complete His forgiveness is.* This results in a deeper love for Christ and a greater commitment to live in obedience to Him. Praise God that His truth overcomes Satan's lies.

Jesus has destroyed all the works of the Devil by living a sinless life and bearing our sin on the cross. Jesus says that He has kept the Father's commands and proves it by rising from the dead. He faced the judgment seat of the Father and was found sinless. Jesus always lived His life in perfect obedience to the Father. Often, we think of this in terms of obeying the Law of Moses. He never lied, lusted, worshipped false gods, etc. But Jesus' obedience was much greater than only obeying the Law of Moses. Jesus obeyed the will of the Father as well by denying His rights. "And being found in human form, he humbled himself by becoming obedient to the point of death, even death on a cross" (Phil. 2:8). The Son chose to obey the Father so that salvation could be given to us. His perfect obedience allowed Him to abide in the love of the Father and bear fruit by fulfilling the Father's plan of salvation.

When we confess our sins and live again in obedience to Him, we eliminate the barrier to Christ's love flowing through us. Our desires become the same as God's desires for us and we joyfully choose to obey. Obedience is always connected to love; it's the motivation behind our obedience. This love is a *decision* to live a life of self-denial no matter the cost. Obedience is our response to the grace that Christ as given sinners like us. We want to fulfill His desire which is that all people may be saved. As He leads, we make sacrifices for His glory, denying ourselves daily and bringing the gospel to those who have not yet received Christ. Are you abiding in His love or living under guilt?

Overflowing Joy

These things I have spoken to you, that my joy may be in you, and that your joy may be full.

– JOHN 15:11

Read Hebrews 12:1-4

Self-denial. Humility. Surrender. These are themes that are repeated throughout John 13-17, and are not ones that typically bring images of joy to mind. Instead, they imply difficulties, suffering, and discomfort. However, it's the world that sends us the message that suffering is bad. The world continually tells us to seek our own self-interests and a comfortable lifestyle, but that's not God's way of discipleship. The way of God is the way of the cross. Just look at Jesus. Qualities such as self-denial and humility bring us closer to the Lord. When we abide in Him, we will enjoy closer fellowship with God. Satan is always trying to destroy this fellowship, because he knows that when we abide in Christ, we will see him for what he truly is—evil.

It's important to remember that even when we are abiding in Christ's love, we will continue to experience trials of many kinds. But we can experience joy in spite of our circumstances as we proclaim the gospel. For instance, we might move from place to place sharing the gospel. When we enter a new community, we may face difficult challenges from the people there. Often challenges might arise when people put their faith in Christ. But after we go through this difficult process and God gives fruit in this unreached place, joy will fill our hearts. Lots of joy. Full joy. Subsequently, we will quickly forget about the trials that greeted us in that place. Tears may fall down our cheeks because of the trials we experienced in that place, but all will be forgotten—the suffering, the conflicts, the struggles—when the lost are found by Christ. Now, because we know that heaven is rejoicing with us, real joy fills our hearts. Full joy is experienced through our struggle to proclaim the gospel.

As He faced His upcoming death on the cross, Christ experienced great suffering in Gethsemane saying to Peter, James and John: "My soul is very sorrowful, even to death" (Mark 14:34). Jesus was arrested, mocked, beaten, and tried unjustly. Then his guards humiliated Him: a crown of thorns was placed on His head, He was given a reed to hold as a scepter, and a scarlet robe was draped over his shoulders. They set Him upon a "throne" and the Roman guards mockingly bowed before Him saying: "Hail, King of the Jews!" (Matt. 27:30)! After that, they nailed Him to a cross, where He suffered excruciating pain. When we pause to consider the suffering of Christ on that day, we should be taken aback to read that Jesus "who for the joy that was set before him endured the cross" (Heb. 12:2). *Jesus is our example of the overflowing joy that awaits those who are faithful, and endure as they bring salvation to others.*

In Luke 15, we also read about three lost items: sheep, a coin, and a son. Actually, the parable of the lost son is really about two lost sons. Both have no love for their father in their hearts, but the father is still seeking them. When he sees the lost younger son return home, he runs out to welcome him. When the older son will not join the celebration held for his brother's return, the father leaves the party to find him and begs him to come into the house to celebrate. After each of these lost items are found, there is great rejoicing in the hearts of those who find them. This is Jesus' point. He, too, was filled with joy when He completed the Father's plan of salvation. When we take part in God's plan of salvation by proclaiming the gospel to others, that same joy is given to us. The full, overflowing joy of heaven fills our hearts when a sinner receives Christ. *Proclaiming the gospel is the means of experiencing joy.* Instead of focusing on the trials we are facing, let's be filled with the joy of Jesus through spreading the gospel. Are you experiencing full joy?

Love One Another

This is my commandment, that you love one another as I have loved you. Greater love has no one than this, that someone lay down his life for his friends.

– JOHN 15:12-13

Read I John 3:11-18

God is love (I John 4:8). God has shown us His true character by through the most magnificent demonstration of His love. Jesus' death on the cross showed us the true meaning of love. Love is the giving of yourself to others. Jesus bore our sins on the cross; He died a horrific death not because He was guilty of breaking God's Law, but because He, the only perfect one, was paying our penalty. Jesus set us free from the penalty of our sins. Jesus suffered, bled, and died showing us how much He loves us. His desire is for us to be with Him throughout eternity. No love is greater than what Christ demonstrated through His death on the cross. Jesus loves us in spite of our sin. He is fully aware of the deficiencies of our character. He knows our pasts and the wrongs we have committed. Yet, He doesn't discard us. Even though Peter denied knowing Christ three times, because it could have cost him his life, Jesus still loved him. Jesus was willing to pay with His life, because He loves us.

If this is the greatest expression of love, how are we to respond? First, by worshipping Christ because this is *our way* of expressing our love for Him. If we love Him, then we are willing to obey His commands. This, too, is worship. We present ourselves as a living sacrifice by obeying Christ, rather than living for the world. Second, we respond by loving one another. If Christ, knowing the sins we have committed and the problems in our character, was willing to die for us, then how much more should we be willing to love those who are our brothers and sisters in the faith? By doing so, we are testifying to the world that we are all the same—sinners saved by the grace of God.

To love one another the way that Jesus loved us is a daunting task. Jesus shows us that love is not an emotion or empty words. It's self-sacrificing action. No doubt, the church is a group of people who have problems; they are sinners who are struggling to live as saints. But by condemning our weak brothers and sisters, we show them that we are no better than the Pharisees, who were hypocrites. Instead, we are to help them grow to maturity. When we are weak, our brothers and sisters can help us so we don't fall into sin. When we go astray, they are also there to lead us back to the one true path. When we are confused or afraid, they are there to strengthen us. We cannot survive the attacks of Satan and the world without the love of our brothers and sisters.

You and your church have an important calling to fulfill, and God has placed you in your specific location to bear fruit. He is working through each member of the church to make known the glory of His name. *Our love for one another is a tool in God's hand used to prune the body of Christ so they will bear much fruit.* We cannot fulfill our calling without the help of the church to spur us on to love and good deeds (Heb. 10:24). Yet, sadly, we are often afraid that if we share our sins and struggles with others, we will be shamed or that our failings will become the source of gossip. Instead of getting the support we need to bear fruit, we hide our sins and struggle in silence. Worse yet, we do the same with Christ. We are afraid to confess our sins to Him, because we think that He will reject us and withdraw His love, but nothing is further from the truth. Christ accepts us as we are. And as we understand the depths of His love for us, we can confess our sins to Him and to each other, knowing that His grace is greater than our sins. Our churches should be safe places for people to share their sin struggles. And our love for one another should be an extension of Christ's love for us. How are you helping others grow into maturity?

No Shortcuts

You are my friends if you do what I command you.

– JOHN 15:14

Read I Samuel 15:1-23

God wants us to bear fruit by involving ourselves in His work of bringing the gospel to the world. To do that, each disciple must be committed to serving with a humble heart and willing to deny himself. We must choose who we will serve daily. It's easy for us to say that we will put God first, but when we are in a difficult situation, we tend to look out only for ourselves. At times like this, we immediately seek a way out instead of trying to understand God's plan.

Many believers are faithful to God when their lives are going smoothly, but can take matters into their own hands when facing trials. They decide not to patiently wait for God's assistance. *I am convinced that people decide to act on their own instead of waiting for God to act, because they don't believe that God's plan is best for them.* They don't believe that God is good. If I am certain that God's plan is perfect and that He works for my good, then I will receive whatever happens with a thankful heart, because I know that my Father loves me and is personally watching over me. For instance, some don't want to move to another place to proclaim the gospel because the people there are from another culture or there are no modern facilities such as malls. And to top it off, the wells have no water during the dry season for bathing and washing clothes. Because of selfish considerations such as these, people won't obey God's calling to bring the gospel to these places.

These situations expose the root of our selfishness— our belief that God neither loves us or His plans for us are good. We resort to finding our own place to serve where our family can be comfortable and have prospects for a better future. *Remember, there are no shortcuts in serving God, there is only the way of the cross.* You can always be confident that the

Father loves you.

I have a friend that started a scholarship program for kids who could not pay their school fees. He hired another believer to administer the program. The believer met with the scholarship recipients each month and distributed the school fees. However, the believer's personal spending was more than the salary he was receiving, so he started stealing money from the scholarship fund to make up the difference. When the theft was discovered, he defended himself by saying: "Just as David took the bread of presence from the altar in the Tabernacle when he fled from Saul because he needed it, I took the money because I need to eat." How distressing when believers cleverly attempt to justify their sin by using Scripture. This is exactly what the Pharisees did also.

My greatest sorrow in serving God is that when people commit sins, they are unwilling to confess them. I don't understand why we are not willing to repent. We all sin. When you do, humble yourself before God instead of defending yourself, blaming others, and manipulating God's Word to justify your sin. Repentance will be easier if you remember that the Father prunes the branches for the good of the branches. Even though it doesn't feel like it, He does it because He loves you. God has a plan to produce much fruit through us, but because we don't believe His plan is best for us, we can fall into the trap of using our own cleverness to do it our way. Repentance is something we need to do daily. The Lord always has a place in ministry for those who know how to repent, because He is the God who forgives. Peter sinned by denying Christ not once, but three times, and Jesus forgave him and restored him to his position as the leader of the apostles. You can completely trust in the Lord's love for you when you confess your wrongs. Leaning on your own schemes will only lead to hypocrisy, and hypocrites will not be blessed by the Lord. Do you believe that God's plans are best for you?

Grow in Maturity

No longer do I call you servants, for the servant does not know what his master is doing; but I have called you friends, for all that I have heard from my Father I have made known to you.

– JOHN 15:15

Read I Corinthians 3:9-15

The goal of our faith is to grow into maturity in Christ Jesus. Paul wrote that as we gaze upon the glory of Christ, we are transformed into His image (II Cor. 3:18). In other words, as we learn to abide in Christ day by day, we will be transformed becoming more like Him. When we first believed in Christ, we were redeemed or ransomed, which means Jesus bought us and we became His slaves. When a slave was bought in the market, he became the property of his new master. Likewise, because Christ purchased us with the payment of His precious, holy blood, we now belong to Him.

Our redemption, however, was only the beginning. The more we abide in Christ, the more we will understand the Father's plan of salvation for the world. In His Word, we see that God desires that no one be condemned. He wants all to be saved through faith in Christ. When we follow Christ, He changes our minds and hearts to be one with His, so that His mission will become our mission. When that happens, we are no longer called slaves but servants. A slave does a job without knowing why, and only does what he is told. However, we understand the Father's plan. We know how much He loves the world and wants it to be set free from Satan's power. *Now that we understand that, we don't hesitate to participate in His mission of bringing the gospel of salvation to the ends of the earth.* We are no longer servants, but now are Christ's friends. Now obeying His will has become our desire. We are God's co-workers for building His kingdom.

119

To have your status changed from slave to friend, there is one requirement that must be fulfilled: to *obey* Christ's commands. Jesus has already revealed the Father's will to us through His Word, so we know what His commands are, but it is the mature disciple who obeys them. Disciples joyfully pay the price to fulfill God's will for them. And Jesus commissioned us to do the work of bringing the gospel to others. He commands us to love one another, so that we will be a witness to the world. By loving one another, people will see that we are no longer enemies of God, but are at peace with Him. And because of that, we can now be at peace with one another as an expression of our love for God.

If we are willing to be pruned by God and to love one another in accordance with Christ's command, we will grow in maturity and God will call us friends. A mark of our maturity is our love for others. If you go to the market, you will probably see a child tugging at their parent's clothes. "Buy me some ice cream," the child might say. If the child's request is not met, the child might throw himself down on the pavement, kicking and screaming. In the child's mind, the whole world is there to love and serve him. But when the child becomes a teenager, the child's love changes. Hopefully, that love is now directed towards a special someone. Upon growing into adulthood, that love transforms into mature love. Now that same child as an adult is willing to sacrifice for those he loves such as his wife and children, because he's grown up and matured. The same is also true in our lives. The more we grow into spiritual maturity, the more we will understand God's love for the world and be thinking of others before ourselves. It will be easy for us to surrender and be used to take the gospel to others, because we want them to know Christ like we do. If you are Christ's friend, you must also love the world as Christ does—with a love that is willing to sacrifice yourself for the salvation of those still in darkness. In what areas of your faith do you need to grow in maturity?

Chosen to Bear Fruit

You did not choose me, but I chose you and appointed you that you should go and bear fruit and that your fruit should abide, so that whatever you ask the Father in my name, he may give it to you.

– JOHN 15:16

Read II Timothy 2:1-10

It's a great honor and blessing to be chosen by God. Even though we were once rebels rejecting Him, He loved us and called us to Himself, giving us salvation through Jesus Christ. We are no longer enslaved by our sins and under the authority of Satan. Before Christ, our debt of sin was increasing every day. There was no way that we could free ourselves from the penalty of the sin we were under, death and destruction were waiting for us. But God did what no other could do: He chose us. He *paid* our debt. He did all of it because of His great love for us. Now we can live with Him forever.

Not only did God desire us by choosing us for salvation, He also set us apart. He chose us for a special service. *Our salvation is not the goal; giving glory to God's name is the goal.* Our salvation is just one step in fulfilling God's plan to glorify His name through the redemption of those held captive by Satan. The second step is participating in His mission. Jesus clearly tells us what that mission is: We are to go, bear fruit, and have fruit that abides. Our mission is not completed when we bear fruit. It is only completed when the fruit that we bear abides in Christ for themselves. The fruit of our ministry must abide in Christ just as we abide in Christ.

All believers are on a mission. We have been chosen to go out into the world for Christ. As we abide in Christ, His life will flow through us so that we produce fruit. Our words and actions should point people to Christ, so they too might confess their sins and become children of God. Our going should directly result in visible fruit. As we do the greater works that Jesus promised us (John 14:12), many will come to faith in Christ. It's our witness that draws them to salvation in Christ.

Believing in Christ is different from joining a club. It's not a matter of being a member, it's having a spiritual rebirth. When we hear the gospel, the Spirit of God works in our heart, so we are convicted of our sins and bow at Christ's feet in worship of our Great Redeemer. God will call people to Himself for salvation, when we carry out God's mission His way. We are not to be bearing fruit through our own trickiness or creativity. To do so, would result in fruit that's not abiding and is eventually cutoff. When we proclaim God's Word, we can have confidence that Jesus will use it to draw people to Himself.

When someone responds to the gospel, they become a new branch abiding in the vine, and the life of Christ begins to flow through them. They realize that their salvation wasn't the goal. Now they will have a desire to see God glorified as a result of many coming to faith in Christ. They, too, are to do the works that Jesus did by proclaiming God's salvation to the lost. *Our mission is all about multiplication. We go, we bear fruit, and this fruit abides. Through abiding, this new fruit goes forth and bears fruit which will in turn abide.* This is how the gospel has spread throughout the world and how it will continue to spread in your area. Making disciples that will abide in Christ is God's plan to fill the world with His glory.

We must boldly ask God that we bear fruit and that this fruit abides in Christ. Pray about this today, because it's God's will. Ask the Father in Jesus' name to give you disciples that will multiply. All the resources of heaven are available to you, so that you will bear much fruit and do greater works than Jesus did. Don't stop asking until God gives you fruit that will abide and that many will come to faith in Christ through the ministry that you do. Is the fruit of your ministry abiding in Christ?

Choosing to Love

These things I command you, so that you will love one another. If the world hates you, know that it has hated me before it hated you.

– JOHN 15:17-18

Read I John 4:7-21

When we are under attack, our flesh wants to strike back. It's natural for us to want to defend ourselves when we feel that we have been wronged. Although the world hates us and wants to do us harm, the gospel clearly teaches us that striking back this is not Jesus' will. In fact, Peter writes: "For it is better to suffer for doing good, if that should be God's will, than for doing evil" (I Pet. 3:17). Sometimes God wills that we suffer, so that through our suffering, we testify to the power of the gospel. Christians throughout the ages have suffered because they confessed Jesus Christ is Lord. The early Christians, for example, were rounded up and fed to lions. The Apostle Paul was arrested and held in a hideous Roman prison. He was eventually martyred, because of his confession that Jesus Christ is Lord. While awaiting His death, Paul wrote to Timothy urging him to stay faithful to the gospel: "for which I am suffering, bound with chains as a criminal" (II Tim. 2:9). The world so hated Christ that Paul had been labeled a criminal, and put in the same category as murders, thieves, swindlers, etc.

Jesus' words juxtapose two reactions to Christ: the world hates Christ, but we love Christ. Christ is always the dividing line. *No one can stay neutral concerning Christ. They will either confess Him as Savior, Redeemer, and Lord, and thereby submit to His rule over their lives, or they will oppose Him.* Satan opposed Christ. He stirred up the Jews against Christ so that the city of Jerusalem shouted: "Crucify him," when given the option to free Jesus from captivity. Satan used the powers of the religious and political establishment in killing Jesus. And what did Jesus do to deserve such a punishment? Nothing.

He never sinned against anyone. Jesus was hated by this world simply because this world is under the authority of Satan, the Adversary (I Pet. 5:8). But, because Christ has been set us free from Satan's grip, we should no longer think in a worldly manner. We should obey His commands and carry out the work that He has appointed us to do rather than fight our persecutors.

The world hates Christ. We know this because of how they exhibit that hatred with us. The same hatred that drove Satan to stir the Jews up in rebellion against Christ is now directed towards us. As Christ's kingdom advances, Satan and the world will work in tandem to oppose us at every turn. Just look around: people are denied work and/or education, beaten, imprisoned, and bullied simply because they love Christ. They are treated in the same manner that Paul was treated—as a common criminal. The world hates us because it hates Christ. But we love one another because we love Christ. *Our attitude towards Christ—hatred or love—is evident by all in the way we treat others.* This is our testimony to the world: as we love others, the world will know that we love Christ. They will know we are Christians by our love!

To love is a command. When we're being mistreated, we have a choice: to respond with Christ's love or to respond like the world with hatred and violence. As Christ's followers, we must respond by accepting our suffering, knowing that it is part of God's plan for us. Perfect love will be shown and lasting fruit borne only as we are obedient to Christ. The church should understand what authentic love is. Through Christ's example, we see a love borne out of sacrifice. When our flesh desires to fight back against those who hurt us, we need to remember Jesus' command to love, even our enemies. Love, don't hate. When you experience suffering for the gospel, be patient knowing that God is at work in your suffering to perfect your faith and bring glory to His name. How are you responding?

Eternal Pursuits

If you were of the world, the world would love you as its own; but because you are not of the world, but I chose you out of the world, therefore the world hates you.

– JOHN 15:19

Read Titus 2:11-14

When we think about living in a worldly manner, we tend to define worldliness in outward forms. Worldly people wear mini-skirts, get drunk, or watch inappropriate movies. It's comfortable for us to define people as either inside or outside of our group, based on what we deem to be appropriate behavior. But that's not what the Bible means by "the world". It has a much deeper meaning. The world is humanity's outlook apart from God, and how their thoughts and actions are enslaved to Satan. Being part of the world means to give allegiance and conform to the pattern of this age. The world is the evil system which deceived us into thinking that people are gods. It's based on the principle that good people go to heaven and bad people go to hell. Many think if they're religious and diligent in performing their external religious duties, they will make themselves good enough to enter paradise. And, the world teaches that people's opinions are just as equally valid as the opinions of God. It redefines sin as mistakes you make that can easily be corrected by a little remorse. But as we know, Judas was remorseful after selling Jesus, yet his remorse could not remove his sin.

Because we are not of this world, we must reject the temporal and material things that can ensnare our hearts in sinful pursuits. Instead, we live for that which is eternal and spiritual. Our decisions and actions need to reflect God's priorities. "The wisdom of this age" (I Cor. 2:6-9) is a deception that can no longer be followed. Nothing that the world offers us can solve our problem of sin. The world tells us to put our hope in the tremendous technological advances yet our hearts are still enslaved to sin. Or we fall sway to the world's deception that wealth and prosperity will solve our problems. "The rich(es) of this present age" (I Tim. 6:17) can cause us to trust in other things rather than in the Giver. The world uses wealth to numb us to the reality that those who follow the world are under judgment.

We need to take our example from the "Lord Jesus Christ, who gave Himself for our sins to deliver us from this present evil age" (Gal. 1:4). Jesus didn't live for earthly comforts, and He didn't think anyone could save themselves through their good works. He *knew* that there was no other way to redeem those loved by God except by giving of Himself as a sacrifice for sins. In doing so, He destroyed the power of Satan over us so we can live in light of eternity instead of being enslaved to sin. Now we are Christ's. He has ransomed us. And when the world sees what He did, the world reacts—and at times violently so. They cannot stand to lose one of their own. The world doesn't want to accept that Christ has defeated Satan, so the world hates us because we have given our allegiance to Christ and not to the world.

Christ has prepared us for the world's response. While He doesn't remove us from the world, He sends us out into this hostile environment to *bear fruit*. Why? Because angry people also need to hear the gospel. In fact, the context of our ministry is adversity. *We can confidently go into the world because we know that Jesus' love will defeat the world's hatred.* Be clear about this: It's not easy to bear fruit. The sun is hot and bears down on the vine and its branches, but as long as the life of the vine flows through the branches, they will not wilt in the heat. All the hatred of the world was poured out on Christ as He was crucified, but He came forth from the grave victorious—His resurrection power is with us as we face the world too. Are you following the example of Christ or are you giving in to the world's deceptions?

Expect Persecution

Remember the word that I said to you: "A servant is not greater than his master." If they persecuted me, they will also persecute you. If they kept my word, they will also keep yours.

– JOHN 15:20

Read Acts 26:9-20

Throughout His final instructions to His disciples, Jesus stressed that humility is one of the keys to being in Christ and producing fruit that lasts. As He did earlier (John 13:16), Jesus reminds them that they are not greater than He is. Our model of humility is Christ Himself who left heaven to come to earth as a servant, and seek and save the lost. He suffered great humiliation as He bore our curse on the cross. Christ, who was in heaven, was willing to subject Himself to all of this because of His humility and willingness to fulfill the Father's plan. In the same way, we too must embrace humility. Bringing the gospel to the world cannot be done with heart full of pride. For it is not our agenda that is our priority. No. We orient our life around God's plans and submit to His perfect will for our lives. There should be no argument from us. If Christ was willing to do the Father's will at such a great cost to Himself and, if we are not as great as Christ, then we too should be willing to do so.

The consequence of living in humble submission to the will of God is persecution. Jesus was persecuted. He was falsely accused and found guilty in spite all of the evidence that proved His innocence. They treated Jesus as though He was a common criminal. They battered and bruised His body. Then they killed Him in one of the cruelest methods ever designed by humans. Christ died on the cross in agony. Yet Jesus faced this persecution with love—for us. He stayed true to the Father's plan knowing that He would be glorified in the end.

Since the death of Christ until now, His followers have

suffered because of their allegiance to Him. "Remember the word that I said to you: 'A servant is not greater than his master.'" In 64 A.D., the Emperor Nero wanted to rebuild a section of Rome, so he set the homes and buildings on fire. The fire was so great that it burned for six days. As expected, the people of Rome were furious that their homes were destroyed. They rightly blamed Nero for starting the fire. In order to save himself, Nero accused the Christians of starting the fire and, by doing so, unleashed a terrible wave of state-sponsored persecution against the church. Christians were arrested and some were crucified, while others were tied to poles and lit on fire. Still, others were brought to the Coliseum where they were made sport of by being fed to lions and tigers. Even the apostles Paul and Peter were swept up in these persecutions and killed.

The witness of the early church was so tied to their persecution and death that the Greek word for witness (martus) became synonymous for martyrs, meaning those who are willing to die for their cause. We are to be ambassadors for Christ, and represent His kingdom to the world. As we faithfully proclaim His message no matter the cost to us personally, we can be confident that our suffering is not fruitless. *The gospel, when served up to the world, even through persecution, means salvation for those appointed by God.* Some will hear and will respond violently by persecuting you; they will think that they are doing a great service to God. But be encouraged: there will be others who will hear and recognize that the Good News is the voice of the Lord calling them to Himself (John 10:27). They will respond not with hatred, but with obedience. What price are you willing to pay so that the gospel will be proclaimed in your area?

Ignorant of God

But all these things they will do to you on account of my name,
because they do not know him who sent me.

– JOHN 15:21

Read John 8:31-47

Jesus not only prepares His disciples for the cruel persecution that will befall them, but He also identifies the root cause of that persecution. He says it's because people do not know the true God. Instead of worshipping Christ, they have designed other gods to worship. Although these gods may no longer be made from wood or stone, people today are still making idols—idols that people can manipulate into doing what they desire. These idols are often crafted in our minds. John Calvin says that the unbelieving heart is a "perpetual factory of idols." Calvin explains, "Man's mind, full as it is of pride and boldness, dares to imagine a god according to its own capacity; …is overwhelmed with the crassest ignorance, it conceives an unreality and an empty appearance as God" (Institutes, I.XI.8). Jesus' claim to being the one true God confronts modern-day idolaters who reject the truth and persecute disciples, so as to protect their false gods.

Knowing God is only possible through Jesus Christ. He is the Word incarnate given to us to reveal God. When demons were in the presence of Christ, they immediately recognized Him and cried out, "You are the Son of God" (Luke 4:41)! Even the demons were familiar with Jesus, but they didn't know Him. (To know Him is to have a relationship with Him.) The demons rejected Christ's rule over them when they rebelled and were consequently cast out from heaven. However, knowing God via a personal relationship with Christ ushers us into the Kingdom of God. Jesus prayed for His disciples saying, "And this is eternal life, that they know you the only true God, and Jesus Christ whom you have sent" (John 17:3). Jesus revealed the Father by showing us that we can enter paradise only through Christ.

Jesus entered history in order to reveal the Father to us. Those who reject Jesus, reject the Father. Throughout His earthly ministry, Jesus was confronted by the religious leaders who rejected His claims about being God incarnate. They would not believe because the God that was being revealed in Jesus was not compatible with the idols that their minds had created. The Jews had the truth found in the Old Testament, so they were familiar with God's promise that the Messiah would come to set them free and reign as the Son of David (II Sam. 7:16). As they suffered under the rule of the pagan Romans, the Jews were longing for the Messiah to come and return the nation of Israel to the Jews. They wanted a God that was a political conqueror. Instead, Christ came as a humble servant who would die to pay the penalty for their sins. Their false understanding of God (i.e. idol) was a result of their own ignorance.

Now Jesus' presence was forcing them to make a choice. Would they turn from their idols and worship God or would they reject Christ and hold on to their idols? The Jews chose their man-designed god and rejected Christ. They showed that they didn't know the Father who sent Christ (John 8:19). Christ still loved them and sent His disciples into Jerusalem and Judea to proclaim the Good News of salvation anyway. *So, too, must we remember that, although the world is persecuting us out of their ignorance about God, the gospel must still be proclaimed.* God is sending us into hostile places not with weapons of war, but with words of hope and actions of love. We have the incredible privilege of telling the world about Christ's death and resurrection. Like Jesus, we can pray for our enemies so that they will come out of their ignorance and turn to the living Christ. How are you responding to those who are ignorant of God?

Jesus Reveals the Father

If I had not come and spoken to them, they would not have been guilty of sin, but now they have no excuse for their sin. Whoever hates me hates my Father also.

– JOHN 15:22-23

Read Romans 1:18-32

The world doesn't know God even though they have been told about Him. God has been actively revealing Himself through creation, the conscience, and Christ. Creation declares God's glory (Ps. 19:1). Our consciences were created to know God's Law since it is written on our hearts (Rom. 2:15). Enough evidence has been provided so that we can recognize the one true God. Even though we have enough evidence that the Father sent the Son into the world, Jesus' coming was a grace of God given to us so that we might know the truth and worship God. "For God did not send his Son into the world to condemn the world, but in order that the world might be saved through him" (John 3:17). *Jesus fully revealed God so that the world would be given every possible means to know God.*

Unfortunately, the world has not turned from its sin. Instead, it has rejected God's revelation, the Lord Jesus Christ, and so are without excuse any longer for their guilt. No one can stand before God and defend themselves saying that they didn't know. Christ's words have eliminated that excuse once and for all. Ever since the Fall, people have used a myriad of excuses to justify themselves. However, these excuses are only offered up as cover for the root problem: they love their sins more than Christ and have rejected the light. Christ's coming exposed sin, and His words cut through to the heart. The world is now even more guilty before God, because they have rejected His final revelation; they have rejected the one and only way of salvation for there is none other that can forgive sins.

When a witness to the truth is given, the hearer of that truth now bears personal responsibility for how they respond to that truth. Jesus has already referred to branches that are cut off and destroyed in the fire, because they are dead. Judas was a dead branch, for example, because He heard Jesus' teachings. Judas should have known that the kingdom that Jesus was establishing was a spiritual kingdom that was to come into the hearts of those who repent. But Judas rejected Jesus' words and was condemned by God. The Jewish religious and political leaders are another type of dead branches. When they heard the words of Christ, they didn't repent either. Instead, they twisted His words and used them as proof that Jesus should be put to death (Mark 14:56-57). Their rejection of Christ's words resulted in God's judgment against them. Sin is not just breaking the Law of God, because it only partially reveals the true God. The complete revelation of God is found in the Lord Jesus Christ. To reject Him is the ultimate sin; dead branches were cut off and burned in the fire, permanently destroyed.

The rejection of the Lord Jesus by the Jewish religious and political leaders was not a surprise to God. In fact, it was part of the Father's plan so that the gospel would be proclaimed to the whole world. "Through their trespass salvation has come to the Gentiles, so as to make Israel jealous" (Rom. 11:11). God's plan was to save the Gentiles through the Jewish leaders' rejection of Christ. This in turn would cause the Jewish people to be jealous so that they, too, would receive the gospel and worship Christ. The Jews hated Jesus and they hated God, but Jesus gave His life for them. *Remember, God loves those who hated Him. Therefore, we should love and bless those who persecute us.* There is no better blessing than to tell even our persecutors about the Good News of Jesus Christ. Who do you need to bless with the Good News today?

Stumbling Block

If I had not done among them the works that no one else did, they would not be guilty of sin, but now they have seen and hated both me and my Father. But the word that is written in their Law must be fulfilled: "They hated me without a cause."

– JOHN 15:24-25

Read I Peter 2:4-12

Jesus performed many miracles. In the Gospel of John, we read that He turned water into wine, healed a man who was lame for 38 years, calmed the sea, fed thousands of people with five loaves of bread and two fish, healed a man born blind, and raised Lazarus from the dead. Jesus did things that no other human could do. These miracles testified that Jesus is Lord, but instead of accepting these signs revealing who Jesus is, the Jews rejected them. The average Jew was attracted to these miracles, because they hoped to gain personally from them. They recognized that Jesus had the power over illness and even death, so they brought their sick to Jesus for healing. Crowds were attracted to Jesus and followed Him wherever He went. On one occasion the crowds needed food, so Jesus fed them with bread that came down from heaven. The Jews last ate bread from heaven when Moses was leading the people in the wilderness. This miracle fascinated the crowds so they immediately wanted to make Jesus their king (John 6:14-15), but Jesus rejected their desire because He came to do the work of the Father.

The leaders came to Jesus asking for a sign. They had rejected all the previous signs that Jesus was the Son of God, so Jesus knew that no matter what He did, the sign would also be ignored. He told them, "No sign will be given... except the sign of the prophet Jonah" (Matt. 12:39). Jesus would prove His authority by going into the stomach of the earth for three days and then rise again. Sadly, even with this sign, they still rejected Him. The Centurion, who oversaw the crucifixion of Christ, was: "filled with awe and said, 'Truly this was the Son of God!'" (Matt 27:54). Yet, the Jewish leaders rejected this sign and instead covered up the resurrection by bribing the guards to lie about what happened (Matt. 28:12-13).

The religious and political leaders also rejected the signs that Jesus gave. They held their religious customs as more important than God's will. That's why, when Jesus healed on the Sabbath, they conspired to kill Him (Matt. 12:14). In spite of all the signs that Jesus gave them, these leaders hardened their hearts instead of humbling themselves before God. *The signs that demonstrated the authority of Jesus became a stumbling block to faith in Jesus.* In order for them to reject these obvious signs, they needed to come up with an alternative explanation for these miracles. Finally, they accused Jesus of performing these signs by the power of the prince of demons (Matt. 12:24). No matter what sign was given, the religious and political leaders chose to deny them even though they always pointed to the Son of God.

The reason they rejected Christ is given in Psalm 69:4. They hated Christ without cause. This was a fulfillment of the prophecy concerning Christ's death. *The world has rejected Christ, because they have rejected the Father, but God's plans were not derailed.* The Father knew of the Jews' rejection of the Son, and He used this rejection to bring salvation to others. Even today, the world rejects God, and many are kept from the truth by leaders who hate the Father and the Son. Others hate Christ because He doesn't perform magic for them every time they need something. In spite of this, God's plan is still moving forward. The death of Christ reminds us that God is still in control. No matter how much hatred and persecution is aimed at us, Christ's kingdom will continue to advance, and His servants will testify to the truth that Jesus is Lord. How are you doing the greater works despite people's rejection of God?

Don't Give Up on Them

But when the Helper comes, whom I will send to you from the Father, the Spirit of truth, who proceeds from the Father, he will bear witness about me.

– JOHN 15:26

Read II Corinthians 4:1-6

God never gives up on the world. In spite of their hatred towards the Father, their rejection of the Son, and their persecution of the church, God has a plan to draw the lost to Himself. God knew that Satan would oppose Christ and His church. "The god of this world has blinded the minds of unbelievers, to keep them from seeing the light of the gospel of the glory of Christ" (II Cor. 4:4). We are in a spiritual battle, and God's response to the world's rebellion and hatred of Him was to send the Holy Spirit. Because this opposition to Christ is spiritual in nature, God sent His Spirit to engage the world so that they will know the truth about the Son.

The Spirit desires that the truth about Christ will be known, believed, and honored by the world. He accompanies the bearers of the gospel as they enter hostile areas and share the Good News. In the very city of Jerusalem where Jesus was crucified, before the very religious leaders that had condemned Jesus to death, Peter proclaimed the resurrection of the Lord Jesus Christ. Peter testified saying, "And we are witnesses to these things, and so is the Holy Spirit, whom God has given to those who obey him" (Acts 5:32). The Spirit of Truth accompanies our gospel presentation so that the testimony of Christ is recognized as true in spite of the opposition.

The mission of the Holy Spirit is clear: The Father has planned the redemption of many for the praise of His glorious name; the Son has completed that plan by dying on the cross to pay our debt of sin so we can be free to live for

Christ, and the Spirit has been sent to apply that salvation on the hearts and minds of those who hear the Good News. And as the Son is sent by the Father, now the Son sends the Spirit. The Spirit is not some impersonal "force," but proceeds from the Father. He is God. *The Father makes available all His own power through the Spirit, so that His plan of redemption will bear fruit.* We can engage in proclaiming the gospel because we know that God is at work convicting sinners of their sin and calling them to repentance.

As the Spirit of Truth, the Holy Spirit reveals the Father and the Son, impressing on people the truth about God and the glory of His plan of redemption. Because people are enslaved to sin and their minds blinded by Satan, they can't recognize Christ, but the Spirit of Truth comes to open their minds. On one occasion, Jesus asked His disciples what conclusions people drew about Him. Then, He asked Peter what his conclusion was. Peter declared that Jesus was the Messiah, the Son of the Living God. To this declaration, Jesus replied, "Flesh and blood has not revealed this to you, but my Father who is in heaven" (Matt. 16:17). The Father revealed the truth about the Son to Peter not through Peter's own logic but through the work of the Holy Spirit. The truth about Christ is known because the Father sent the Holy Spirit to testify about Jesus. The Spirit empowers our testimony so that people will understand the truth about the Son.

Don't be surprised with opposition to your witness because, just as many opposed Christ, they will oppose you as well. The power of our testimony is not limited by the strength of the opposition. No one can shut the door that God is holding open, so we rely not on our clever plans or fancy words. We are engaging in a God-sized endeavor and only He can bring it to a successful conclusion. Rely on the Spirit. Let Him work through you. He will turn even the most resistant hearts towards Christ.

God never gives up on the world. Have you given up on it?

Boldly Proclaim Christ

And you also will bear witness, because you have been with me from the beginning.

– JOHN 15:27

Read II Corinthians 4:7-14

John 15 starts out with abiding in Christ. Although we are not physically with Christ as His disciples were, we are with Him spiritually, and it's our abiding in Him that compels us to act and bear fruit. John 15:27 says, "You also will bear witness." Abiding in Christ and bearing witness are connected with one another. Jesus said that we are in Him and He is in us (John 14:20). If we are abiding in Christ, His life and love will flow through us. We will go and bear fruit, facing a hostile world with full confidence, because as we testify, the Spirit of Truth is at work causing men and women to accept Christ as their Savior and Lord.

Jesus always intended for the gospel to be spread through us, His disciples. Unlike many people, who have founded religions, Jesus never wrote a book. Instead, He left it to His followers to record their testimonies in the form of written books called the Gospels. This is consistent with the intentions expressed by Jesus throughout His earthly ministry. When Jesus first called His disciples, He told them that they would be fishers of men (Matt. 4:19). When He commissioned His disciples, He told them they would be His witnesses (Acts 1:8). Jesus was constantly sending people out to be His witnesses. Just as He did with the Samaritan woman or the man who was possessed by demons, so even now Jesus is sending us out as witnesses.

Witnesses do not make up a story, they simply repeat what they know is true. The disciples were eyewitnesses to Christ's death and resurrection. Many people can claim to know the truth but, in fact, they can actually be fabricating or embellishing the story. This is different from what the disciples did. Peter himself testified that he and the other disciples were eyewitnesses: "For we did not follow cleverly devised myths when we made known to you the power and coming of our Lord Jesus Christ" (II Pet. 1:16). They proclaimed what they had seen and heard (Acts 4:20). And they were willing to suffer and die for this testimony, *because it was true.*

God has commissioned us to do likewise. The Spirit of Truth is given to us so we can give witness to Christ. We can be confident that the message we proclaim, that we read in the gospels, *is true.* And the more we realize the hopelessness of the world's situation and the greatness of God's plan, the more we will be willing to pay the price to "proclaim the excellences of him who called you out of darkness into his marvelous light" (I Pet. 2:9). Proclaiming this to the world means that we must be willing to go. *It means we leave our comforts and safety to go where the darkness is thickest, because we know that the power of the Spirit goes with us.*

Christ's disciples testified about Him. They willingly paid the price to proclaim Christ, even the ultimate price of their very lives. Christ was worth it. After all that He had done, the disciples gave themselves joyfully to the task of bearing witness. While the world wielded fiery arrows towards them, the disciples boldly performed their task, because they knew that Jesus reigns. You, too, can expect opposition from the world—even hatred—but take heart. Some will believe. Fruit will be borne. And it will be worth it! In the midst of great opposition in Corinth, God commanded Paul to keep testifying, "for I have many in this city who are my people" (Acts 18:10). Facing difficulties like these are not easy, but God gives us the courage when we need it. Pray like Paul did, "that words may be given to me in opening my mouth boldly to proclaim the mystery of the gospel" (Eph. 6:19). Paul didn't testify when it was easy or convenient; He knew that as a disciple you testify at all times, but he also had confidence that God was working through his witness to draw many people to Christ. What is keeping you from witnessing more boldly?

Abide and Stand Firm

I have said all these things to you to keep you from falling away.

— JOHN 16:1

Read Matthew 26:47-75

The gospel is God's power to destroy the works of Satan. Satan masterfully manipulates the nations from age to age by creating new deceptions. Different political and economic systems give the appearance of independence from God, yet all of these deceptions result in the same thing: They keep the nations from returning to God and worshipping Him. When the gospel comes, the nations are confronted with the reality that they are not God, and that their devices are but a mere vapor. The true power to change the world is found in Christ. His death and resurrection have won the victory. The amazing truth of this is that this power is in each one of us as we abide in Christ and as we go out into the world to proclaim Jesus Christ is Lord. Through our testimony, the nations will be brought to Christ.

Satan knows that he has lost. He tried to derail Christ's mission but failed when Christ rose from the dead and ascended to His eternal throne. As a result, *Satan has now shifted his strategy to attack the messenger in order to prevent the spread of the gospel.* The tools in his arsenal vary. Satan tempts us to sin so our words are discredited, and we're disqualified to run this race. He also pressures us to live in fear and shame so that we will not proclaim the gospel.

Jesus warned His disciples that they are under the threat of failing. On this night after Judas departed and Jesus finished announcing His imminent arrest and death, Peter began to boast that even though everyone else deserted Jesus, he never would. In response to Peter's boasting, Jesus informed the disciples of the spiritual warfare going on to discredit their witness and render them fruitless. Jesus said to Peter, "Satan demanded to have you, that he might sift you like wheat, but I have prayed for you that your faith may not fail. And when you have turned again, strengthen your brothers" (Luke 22:31-32). Jesus knew that Satan would shift his attacks towards the disciples, and that these attacks would result in some of them falling away. From his prison cell while awaiting death, the Apostle Paul wrote to Timothy, "All who are in Asia turned away from me" (II Tim. 1:15). The Apostle Paul recognized that Timothy, too, might fall away. Satan continues to attack disciples in hopes that he can keep many from hearing the gospel and believing in Christ.

The gospel records the events that happened before and after the arrest of Jesus in Gethsemane. Judas departs into darkness as he goes to sell Jesus, Jesus is arrested, and the disciples flee from Him, leaving Jesus alone in chains. Then the gospel recounts Jesus' faithful and bold testimony during His interrogation by Caiaphas, the High Priest. Finally, we read of Peter's denial of Christ. The contrast could not be clearer. Judas betrayed, Peter denied, and the disciples fled, but Jesus stood firm in His testimony. What differentiates us from the actions of Judas, Peter, and Jesus? *It's abiding.* Jesus is God incarnate; therefore, God's power was fully in Him. Judas was not a believer, so there was no life flowing through him. Peter, on the other hand, would only bear fruit as he humbled himself and abided in Christ. Christ prayed for Peter so that his faith would not fail. Christ also prays for our faith in the midst of Satan's attacks.

Satan's attacks are real and powerful. We cannot withstand them apart from the life of Christ working in us. That's why abiding in Christ is so important. Abiding in Christ is not a slogan to be repeated, but it is our source of strength in fulfilling our calling as disciples. As you live out your calling to make disciples of all peoples, stay connected to Christ, and abide in Him so you won't fall away. Don't give Satan a foothold in your heart. Instead, fill your heart with love for Christ, and let Him dwell richly in you (Col. 3:16). Are you in danger of falling away?

Facing Opposition

They will put you out of the synagogues. Indeed, the hour is coming when whoever kills you will think he is offering service to God. And they will do these things because they have not known the Father, nor me.

– JOHN 16:2-3

Read Acts 22:3-16

Violence done in the name of God is nothing new. The history of religion is filled with examples of those in the majority persecuting those in the minority. And this is still true today throughout the world. However, this isn't what Jesus is telling His disciples; He's not referring to the manipulation of religion for gaining power. He's speaking of a much greater spiritual reality. When we enter into the ministry of making disciples of all peoples, Satan sets himself up in opposition to us. *Satan enlists the world and its systems to oppose the fulfillment of the Great Commission.* He blinds the eyes of the world so they believe that it is their religious duty to oppose Christ and His disciples.

Jesus and His disciples faced hostility from the Jews as the gospel was proclaimed. It is interesting to note that Jesus, His disciples, and Paul all followed a similar ministry pattern. They first brought the gospel to the Jews—some of which received the gospel—but there was opposition that closed the door to ministry among the Jews in that region, so they subsequently took the gospel to the Gentiles. For example, Paul and Barnabas brought the gospel to Antioch in Pisidia, where their ministry faced resistance from the Jews. Therefore, Paul declared: "It was necessary that the word of God be spoken first to you. Since you thrust it aside and judge yourselves unworthy of eternal life, behold, we are turning to the Gentiles" (Acts 13:46). God gave the Jews an opportunity to be the first to hear the gospel. After all, the Messiah and salvation came through Israel. But the gospel was not only for the Jews; disciples were to be made from all nations.

It was the opposition from the Jews that led to the death of Christ. In fact, the Jewish leaders thought they were doing a great service by putting Jesus to death. Caiaphas, the High Priest declared: "it is better for you that one man should die for the people, not that the whole nation should perish" (John 11:50). The Jews also attacked Jesus' disciples. They arrested Peter and John, put James to death by the sword, and stoned Stephen. Hatred towards Christ was so great that more than 40 Jews took an oath not to eat or drink before they ambushed and killed Paul. The Book of Acts tells of the great zeal of the Jews for defending their religion and opposing the gospel.

Paul acknowledges their zeal, but explains the cause of it. In Romans 10:2, he writes that the Jews "have a zeal for God, but not according to knowledge." This is exactly Jesus' point. They do these things in the name of God, but they don't *know* God. If they knew Christ, they would have known the Father. *And because they are blinded to the truth about Christ, their zeal leads them to self-deception.* They believe that they are honoring God by persecuting the gospel messenger when, in fact, they are instruments of Satan. Zeal and sincerity are not enough to prove the truth about your belief. It must be rooted in facts.

We know that Christ is God because He rose again. Therefore, we obey His commands no matter the price we may pay. Obeying His command to proclaim the gospel means that we are *willing* to be in harm's way. And, even if our faith is opposed with violence and fanaticism, we are to respond with love. We follow Christ's example from the Cross when Jesus said: "Father, forgive them, for they know not what they do" (Luke 23:34). We don't meet fanaticism with fanaticism or hatred with hatred. Instead, we obey God out of love by patiently bearing all things for the sake of the gospel. Are you humbly facing your opposition knowing that God will glorify Himself through your testimony?

God's Plan Never Fails

But I have said these things to you, that when their hour comes you may remember that I told them to you. I did not say these things to you from the beginning, because I was with you.

— JOHN 16:4

Read II Timothy 1:8-14

Trusting that God has a plan is essential to being obedient disciples. No matter what we face, we can be confident that Jesus is in control of the situation. In the Great Commission, Jesus promised that His presence would be with us until the end of the age. Therefore, we can confidently face the trials that the world throws at us, because these difficulties were already known to Christ. He told us to expect them, so we are not to be surprised when they happen nor should we complain. This is all part of being obedient to the Great Commission. Jesus was obedient until death in order to fulfill the Father's plan of salvation. We, too, should expect trials as we obey the Father in bringing the gospel to the world.

When Jesus was with His disciples, all the attention was focused on Him, because people were amazed at His miracles and awed by His teaching. For the religious authorities, it was a matter of determining whether or not Jesus was the Messiah. Eventually they concluded that they didn't want the kind of Messiah that Jesus represented. At that point, their attention on Christ moved from mere curiosity to outright hatred. As their opposition to Jesus increased, the religious authorities continued to focus on Jesus only. So for the most part, the disciples were left alone. When they finally arrested Jesus, they let the disciples go, because it was the Father's plan that only Jesus was to die on the Cross that night. The disciples were to be spared so they could become witnesses to all that Jesus said and did.

Now that He was departing, the animosity directed at

Jesus was being directed at His disciples. They would now suffer and be martyred as they bore witness to the resurrection. Jesus understood the great pressure the disciples would face. While He was with them, He could direct the opposition to Himself, but now the disciples had to face the opposition alone, without Him. Jesus didn't want them to fall away, so He told them what was going to happen. Their suffering didn't catch God by surprise. God knew that Satan would attack the gospel messengers. It might be easy for people to look at Jesus' death on the Cross and think that God's plan failed, but then Jesus rose from the dead. Now as the disciples are facing persecution, they might think once again that God's plan was failing. *Don't lose heart. Jesus told us these things would happen so we might know that God has a plan and His plan will not fail.*

Understanding God's timing and being patient for Him to work strengthens us during our trials. Jesus said, "But I have said these things to you... I did not say these things to you from the beginning." Jesus knew that there was an appropriate time to tell His disciples certain things. Even throughout the Scriptures, God reveals His plan of salvation to Israel in an incremental manner. Adam was promised that one of Eve's descendants would crush Satan. Abraham was told that this promised Redeemer would be one of Isaac's descendants. Moses was given the Law and the Tabernacle to teach Israel that without a sacrifice it's impossible to approach God. God didn't give the entire plan of salvation to Adam. Bit by bit God made it known to Israel until, in the fullness of time, Jesus, the Lamb of God, who takes away the sins of the world, came.

When you are undergoing difficulties and pressure because of your witness, be confident that God has a plan and it's being implemented. Although the situation might seem grim, God is powerful and His plan will not fail. He opens prison doors and frees us from the wicked plans of evildoers. Don't despair. Remember that Jesus told us this would happen—it's part of the plan. Will you trust God and His timing?

Seeing the Big Picture

But now I am going to him who sent me, and none of you asks me,
"Where are you going?" But because I have said these things to you,
sorrow has filled your heart. Nevertheless, I tell you the truth: it is to
your advantage that I go away, for if I do not go away, the Helper will
not come to you. But if I go, I will send him to you.

– JOHN 16:5-7

Read Romans 8:9-28

God is glorified when sinners repent and worship Him. Therefore, we want to do greater works because this will result in greater glory for God. As more people turn from their sins, God will be lifted up in the hearts of people from all nations and tribes. The Father made a way for sinners to return to Him through the death and resurrection of the Son. By faith, all who believe, can join together at the throne of God to worship our Redeemer. Jesus' entire focus while on earth was fulfilling the work that the Father had given Him. Now that His work was completed, the Son was to depart and return to heaven.

Jesus' statement that He was going to leave, greatly distressed the disciples. For three years, they had enjoyed the blessings of being with Jesus. They lacked nothing during this period. And, moreover, they were participants in the amazing work of God, but Jesus now said that He was going back to the Father. Understandably, this caused great sorrow for the disciples. They knew what their lives were like before and after meeting Jesus. They didn't want to go back to the way their lives used to be. Yet Jesus told them that it was for their advantage that He went away. This must have been hard for the disciples to comprehend.

Sometimes God's plan brings us personal sorrow. We have an idea of how we would like things to go and it's not going to turn out that way. Many of us have even planned out our lives: where we will live, what we will do, etc., *but being disciples of Christ means we are committed to obeying* His *commands. We must deny ourselves and our personal agendas in order that we might participate in His plan.* Following God's plan means going where He wants us to go and prioritizing His work over our worldly profits. Of course, sorrow over this loss is understandable. At times, we will mourn our losses. We will want to hold on to things in the world, but we realize that God has a plan for us that is greater than anything that we can imagine.

Like the disciples, we don't often understand the bigger picture. The disciples wanted Jesus to stay with them, but Jesus knew that if He didn't go, the Holy Spirit wouldn't come. Jesus was confined to a physical body and could only be in one place, but when the Spirit came, He would indwell all believers as they spread out across the globe. *The greater works of proclaiming the gospel to all people could only be accomplished if Jesus was dwelling through the Spirit in the believers.* The Spirit's indwelling would give believers the power to testify to the resurrection. All believers have access to Jesus' presence as we abide in Christ through the indwelling Holy Spirit. When you think about it, it's to our advantage that Jesus returned to the Father. Now, His power is at work throughout the world through us.

Jesus' disciples didn't understand God's plan, so they were focused on what they believed was most beneficial for themselves, but God always works all things for our good. We might not understand God's plan at the moment, but His plan is always superior to ours. We often resist change because we are comfortable with what we have, but God is asking us to have confidence in Him. Think of His character and His promises whenever you have doubts. God has given you the greatest blessing of all through His presence in the Holy Spirit. The Holy Spirit is given to all who believe, so step out boldly in faith, knowing that any sorrow you might experience is only temporary. Your obedience to God will *always* result in a greater and deeper joy. Are you submitting to His plan?

The Work of The Spirit

And when he comes, he will convict the world concerning sin and
righteousness and judgment: concerning sin, because they do not
believe in me; concerning righteousness, because I go to the Father,
and you will see me no longer; concerning judgment, because the
ruler of this world is judged.

— JOHN 16:8-11

Read Acts 2:22-36

Apart from the power of God working in our hearts, we can't repent of our sins and return to God. The truth is: we are in bondage to Satan and our sinful nature, so God has to work. He has set us free by redeeming us through the precious blood of Jesus (I Pet. 1:18-19). And now as we proclaim the gospel, God works to set captives free from Satan. Convincing someone to follow Jesus is not done through debates or social work, there must be a new birth— a spiritual birth—brought about by the Holy Spirit.

That's why God gave us the Holy Spirit. Our testimony about Christ would be powerless against the power of Satan, except that God's power is at work in the words that we speak. It's the Holy Spirit who convicts the world of sin. He reveals the error of our ways and vindicates Christ. Satan and the world once judged Christ. Then they chose to willfully reject Him as the Messiah, because they wanted a God who could be manipulated so as to gain more earthly power and riches. However, Jesus taught that His kingdom was not of this world. He was interested in restoring the glory and worship due to the Father, rather than achieving secondary matters such as earthly power.

The world manipulated sin, justice, and judgment to condemn Christ. Once the Spirit came, however, all of these things were restored to their proper meaning. Sin is rejecting Christ; the world chose to reject Christ calling Him a sinner (John 9:16, 24). It's the Holy Spirit's job to show the world that they are sinners and to believe in Jesus (John 6:29). Sadly, the world perverted righteousness by unjustly putting Christ to death on the Cross. However, the Father proclaimed Jesus as Lord by raising Him from the dead. God judged Satan at the Cross while lifting Jesus up to His heavenly throne. *In the death and resurrection of Christ, the world's order was completely exposed as a lie by God, and God glorified Himself by destroying the works of Satan.*

Our gospel proclamation, then, is joining with the Holy Spirit to testify to the truth about Christ. Our message should focus on sin, righteousness, and judgment. It's our sin that deepens our debt with God and put us under judgment. The world and all its resources cannot pay off our debt of sin. In fact, it's the world that leads us to hopelessness, but the death and resurrection of Christ is the only way of salvation and hope. The Holy Spirit bears witness to this truth. As Christ's disciples, we are able to shine the light of God into their darkness, so they turn from their sin and reject the deceptions of Satan. Our witness is fueled by abiding in Christ. Furthermore, union with Christ results in the Spirit working through us, so that we can live out the gospel message. The Spirit works in our lives to conform us to the righteous image of Christ. We have overcome the ruler of the world through the blood of Christ.

Without abiding in Christ, we cannot bear witness to the truth about Christ and expose the world for what it is. We are to live holy lives in obedience to God's Word. As we abide in Christ, the fruit of the Spirit becomes ever more evident in our lives, and the world will no longer be able to deny the truth about Jesus, because they will see Him in our lives. People may persecute us, but they will not be able to deny the Spirit of God in our lives and testimonies. To what extent are you allowing the power of God to flow through your life and reveal the truth about Christ?

The Revelation of The Spirit

I still have many things to say to you, but you cannot bear them now.
When the Spirit of truth comes, he will guide you into all the truth,
for he will not speak on his own authority, but whatever he hears he
will speak, and he will declare to you the things that are to come.

– JOHN 16:12-13

Read I Corinthians 2:6-16

Solomon was known for his great wisdom. Yet even though he was wise, Solomon didn't understand God's great plan. He investigated the world and its greatness, but in the end, he could only conclude that everything was meaningless. Death renders all the world's pride and riches completely meaningless. The world has no solution for our final enemy–death. Jesus, however, had wisdom that didn't come from earthly things. Rather, His wisdom came from heaven, for He was the Word of God, which became flesh. Not even someone as great as Solomon could comprehend the depths of this wisdom. Jesus shared glimpses of this heavenly wisdom with His disciples. However, He knew that they were unable to comprehend His teaching. Thus, He sent the Spirit to reveal these truths to them.

What was the great mystery of heaven that could not yet be revealed to the disciples? It was God's plan of salvation. Until the Spirit came, the disciples couldn't understand the need for the Cross, the reality of the resurrection, or their commissioning at the ascension. Even after He rose, Jesus taught His disciples about the kingdom of God, but they couldn't comprehend it. The disciples still thought that the gospel was the restoration of Israel to a place of earthly power, but it was so much more. The wisdom of heaven is "the mystery of his will… which he set forth in Christ as a plan for the fullness of time, to unite all things in him, things in heaven and things on earth" (Eph. 1:9-10). God would unite humanity, both Jews and Gentiles, through faith in

Christ to the praise of His glory.

If the disciples were still struggling with why Jesus had to die on the cross, how would they ever be able to understand the depths of God's wisdom to save all nations through the Messiah? This indeed was too much for the disciples to bear at this time. On the way to Jerusalem where Jesus would be crucified, the disciples were arguing about who was the greatest. Later, the arrest of Christ caused the disciples to scatter. They regrouped days later in a locked upper room. When they were with Christ, they couldn't understand the Father's plan of salvation. Now separated from Christ, the disciples' lack of understanding was compounded by the fear that gripped their hearts.

Full understanding of Jesus' words came after the Spirit arrived. The Spirit did not bring new teachings, but explained what was eternal and implemented the work of salvation. When the Father and the Son prepared the plan of salvation, the Spirit was also there. The details were known by the Father, Son, and Spirit. Even though it was Jesus who fulfilled the Father's plan of salvation, the Spirit was necessary to spread the news of salvation by convicting the world of sin and teaching believers the details of the plan. And just as Jesus only spoke the words that the Father gave Him (John 8:28), so too the Spirit only speaks the words that He hears from God.

Jesus told some Jews that believed in Him, "If you abide in my word, you are truly my disciples, and you will know the truth, and the truth will set you free" (John 8:31-32). *The key to understanding God's Word is to abide in Christ.* As we abide in Christ, it is the Spirit who teaches us the wisdom of God, because the Spirit knows the Father's deepest thoughts and reveals them to God's children. We can trust the Spirit, because He communicates God's truths accurately. We can have full confidence in what we know about Christ, and we can act boldly to proclaim these truths, because we will not be ashamed on the day of judgment. What is the Spirit revealing to you?

The Spirit's Role in The Father's Plan

*He will glorify me, for he will take what is mine and declare it to you.
All that the Father has is mine; therefore I said that he will take what
is mine and declare it to you.*

– JOHN 16:14-15

Read Revelation 5:1-14

All heaven glorifies Christ. Before the throne of God, the angels, the elders, and the nations sing praises to His glory. "Worthy is the Lamb who was slain, to receive power and wealth and wisdom and might and honor and glory and blessing" (Rev. 5:12)! Heaven is filled with songs to the Lamb that was slain, Jesus Christ. Through His obedient suffering, He fulfilled the Father's plan of salvation and paid the debt of sin for all who believe that Jesus Christ is Lord. When Jesus hung on the cross, He was humiliated as one who was accursed, but Jesus committed Himself into the Father's hands, and the Father lifted Him up to glory— *worthy is the Lamb who was slain!*

The plan of salvation didn't end with the ascension of Jesus to heaven. This was only another step in God's master plan to glorify His name. Now that the payment of our debt of sin was completed, the plan shifted to a new phase. News of Jesus' resurrection was to be spread throughout the world so that all would have the chance to hear and respond. One of the Apostle Paul's travelling companions understood this well. Luke wrote, in the beginning of his book, the Acts of the Apostles, that: "In the first book ..., I have dealt with all that Jesus began to do and teach, until the day when he was taken up" (Acts 1:1-2a). The first book, the Gospel according to Luke, recounted the life of Christ from His birth until His ascension. Luke describes this as all that "Jesus began to do and teach." The Book of Acts was the story of what Jesus continued to do and teach after He left this earth. It describes the exploits of the disciples and the early church as they did the greater works of proclaiming the gospel in Jerusalem, Judea, Samaria, and to the ends of the earth. The works that Jesus continued to do came through the work of the Holy Spirit as believers brought the news of the resurrection to the nations.

This was not a new plan, but the continuation of what Jesus did. Jesus was given full knowledge and possession of what the Father has. Now Jesus has taken all of that and has entrusted it to the stewardship of the Spirit. *The Spirit reveals the historical fulfillment of the plan of salvation by Jesus. He helps us to understand it, leads us in the proclamation of it, and applies it to the hearts of sinners.* The closeness of the Father, Son, and Spirit is revealed in the plan of salvation. Jesus revealed the Father, and the Spirit revealed the Son to the disciples. In so doing, the Spirit revealed the Father as well to Jesus' followers. The Father, Son, and Spirit are inter-connected in a level of intimacy that can only be described as oneness.

There is great humility in the inter-connectedness of the Father, Son, and Spirit. The Holy Spirit is humble; He doesn't draw attention to Himself but instead glorifies Christ. The Son is also humble. He went to the Cross in order to glorify the Father. The humility of God is seen in the plan of salvation. As we go out into the world to testify to the death and resurrection of Christ, we are to reflect this humility. The Spirit also declares the truth of Christ to us. What happens? We believe the truth and humble ourselves before it by proclaiming that we are not God. We glorify Christ, because He did for us what nobody on earth could do for themselves. As the Spirit reveals the things of God to us, we grow to appreciate even more greatly the work of Christ on our behalf, and commit ourselves anew to making His great salvation known to the ends of the earth. Are you committed to continuing the things that Jesus began by bringing the gospel to others?

Comprehending God's Wisdom

"A little while, and you will see me no longer; and again a little while,
and you will see me." So some of his disciples said to one another,
"What is this that he says to us, 'A little while, and you will not see
me, and again a little while, and you will see me'; and, 'because I am
going to the Father'?" So they were saying, "What does he mean by 'a
little while'? We do not know what he is talking about.

– JOHN 16:16-18

Read I Corinthians 1:18-31

The disciples often failed to understand Jesus' teaching. For instance, when Jesus told the Parable of the Sower, the disciples needed a private explanation from Jesus to interpret the parable. Often the disciples seemed to be slow to grasp the essence of Jesus' teaching. Now in the moments before Jesus' arrest in the garden, the disciples were once again befuddled. Jesus told them that something was going to happen in "a little while." And "a little while" later, something else was again going to take place. Jesus was going to be gone, and then He was going to reappear. It reminds me of the time I was visiting the home of a shaman. The shaman told me that he often disappears in the middle of talking with someone. He told me that if that happened, I was not to be alarmed as he was certainly still there, although invisible. The shaman was trying to add to his mystique by claiming incredible powers. But Jesus was not talking about playing a shaman's mind game. He was talking about a real, significant event that was about to take place.

Understandably, the disciples were on edge. After all the important teaching that Jesus gave them that night, they seemed most disturbed by Jesus' claim of His imminent departure. After three years of being with Jesus, the disciples had no idea what they would do in such an event, without Jesus. When combined with the heightened excitement in Jerusalem about the Passover Feast, and the overwhelming reception of Jesus, the disciples were on an emotional roller-coaster, but they knew that something big was about to happen in "a little while."

However, the disciples made one colossal mistake. They heard the teachings of Jesus and couldn't understand them, *so instead of seeking understanding from Christ, they tried to interpret Jesus' words themselves.* Jesus had just told them that His words were too much for them to bear and that later the Spirit of Truth would come to guide them in all truth, but they couldn't wait for later. Because Jesus was going to leave "in a little while," they needed to know now! So, the disciples got together to interpret Jesus' words according to what they thought was appropriate. Their interpretation, however, excluded the death of Jesus on the cross.

It shouldn't have surprised the disciples that Jesus was speaking about His death and resurrection because, on many occasions, Jesus foretold these events. But the dull minds of the disciples couldn't comprehend the wisdom of God. Still, today people don't comprehend God's plan of redemption. The world wants to create a Jesus that fits their own view of what the Messiah should say and do. They want a Savior who doesn't demand anything of them, but instead is on call to serve their every need. They don't want to deny themselves. They want to live their own lives with "a little bit" of Jesus added to appease their conscience.

The gospel is not about you. It's about God and His plan to bring ultimate glory to Himself through saving us from our sins. God is most glorified in our salvation, because He did what no one else could do. He defeated Satan and set us free to worship Him. There's no question the gospel places demands on our lives, such as living holy lives and being willing to sacrifice worldly comforts so God's glory will spread throughout the earth, but it's all worth it! Are you trying to comprehend God's plans through your own understanding or are you asking God to reveal His plans to you?

Gaining Perspective Through Prayer

Jesus knew that they wanted to ask him, so he said to them, "Is this what you are asking yourselves, what I meant by saying, 'A little while and you will not see me, and again a little while and you will see me'?"

– JOHN 16:19

Read James 1:2-18

Jesus knows what's on our minds. He knows all of our questions, doubts, and struggles. We might be able to deceive others, since they can only draw conclusions about us from what they observe and hear, but Jesus is different. He knows our thoughts before they are even expressed. Once again, Jesus knows the disciples' thoughts just as He had known the thoughts of others on many occasions. John records that Jesus didn't place His confidence in others, "for he himself knew what was in man" (John 2:25). Jesus instead hoped only in the Father.

The fact that Jesus knows what's in our minds should cause us to live differently. First, we need to start by being honest with ourselves. We may be able to hide our weaknesses and sins from others, but we can't hide them from God. It's always better to respond to the Spirit's work of conviction of sin by confessing them to God, rather than trying to defend ourselves. In the gospel, we learn that there's nothing we can do to make God love us more, and we can't do anything to make Him love us less. God knows our sins; He has paid the debt for these sins.

Our sins can no longer keep us from being children of God, but they can and do affect our fellowship with God. Everything God desires for us is achieved by abiding in Christ. We can't bear fruit without the life of Christ flowing through us, because our sins will hinder fruit in our lives. That's why the Father prunes us. How does He do it? The Spirit reveals our sins to us so that we confess them and humbly receive discipline from the Father (Heb. 12:5-6). When we blame others for our sins and make ourselves out to be victims, we are denying the work of the Spirit in our lives. Abiding in Christ requires a daily practice of confessing our sins and receiving His forgiveness. One way to do this is celebrating the Lord's Supper. Here, we can take a moment to evaluate our hearts to see if they are free from doubt, jealousy, self-righteousness, and any other attitudes that need pruning.

Secondly, the fact that Jesus knows our thoughts should drive us to prayer. Jesus was always honest with His disciples. He told them that they should expect to suffer because of the gospel. We, too, should expect nothing less. Not surprisingly, suffering can cause confusion and doubt to grow in our minds. Our defense against these things is not to rely on our own logic. Our earthly wisdom fails us when we see the wicked prospering and the righteous suffering. The suffering of believers only makes sense when it's viewed through the lens of faith. In Psalm 73, Asaph struggled to understand this dilemma. He admitted that his faith was faltering and nearly failed: "When I thought how to understand this, it seemed to me a wearisome task, until I went into the sanctuary of God; then I discerned their end" (Ps. 73:16-17). *Only through prayer can we gain the perspective that makes sense of why we must suffer for the gospel.*

Prayer gives us access to the wisdom of heaven. James, writing to a church that was suffering because of the gospel, encouraged them to go to the Lord in prayer. He wrote, "If any of you lacks wisdom, let him ask God, who gives generously to all without reproach, and it will be given him" (Jas. 1:5). God is ready to answer us. When we bring our confusion and doubts to Him in prayer, Jesus will reveal the will of the Father to us so that we will stand firm in the midst of trials. Take advantage of this. Don't delay in going to the Lord in prayer. Approach Him with a humble heart, asking Him for wisdom, and to testify of Himself through your sufferings. What is in your heart today that you need to bring before God?

Experiencing Joy

Truly, truly, I say to you, you will weep and lament, but the world will rejoice. You will be sorrowful, but your sorrow will turn into joy. When a woman is giving birth, she has sorrow because her hour has come, but when she has delivered the baby, she no longer remembers the anguish, for joy that a human being has been born into the world. So also you have sorrow now, but I will see you again, and your hearts will rejoice, and no one will take your joy from you.

– JOHN 16:20-22

Read I Peter 4:12-19

No one wants to suffer. It wasn't God's plan for us to toil and suffer pain. This came as a result of the Fall. Interestingly, Jesus talks about suffering using the illustration of childbirth. Eve was cursed with pain in childbirth because of her sin. When all things are made new at the end of time, everything will be fully restored to how God originally intended it to be. God "will wipe away *every* tear from their eyes, and death shall be no more, neither shall there be mourning, nor crying, nor pain anymore, for the former things have passed away" (Rev. 21:4). What a glorious day that will be when there is no longer any pain or death! While that describes the life to come, in this world we will undergo much hardship, because Satan continues to oppose the gospel and the gospel messenger. *Those who obey Christ and proclaim the gospel can expect many trials in this life.*

The disciples, like the rest of the Jews, were looking for a Messiah who would take away their suffering. They were chafing under the Roman occupation and wanted to be set free. Jesus, however, had no desire to be the world's version of the Messiah. His calling was much greater. He was here to fulfill the Father's plan. And in this plan, the Messiah must suffer. In just a few moments, Jesus would be unjustly tried and cruelly put to death on the cross. His suffering would be enormous, but it wasn't only physical suffering. Jesus would also bear our sins while on the cross. The holy Christ was made sin for us in order to pay our debt of sin. With this sacrifice, all of the Father's wrath was poured out on Christ, and only because He alone was infinitely holy could He face the wrath of the Father and not be consumed by it.

We can't imagine the immense pain felt by Christ as He succumbed to Satan's vicious attack. He was beaten, mocked, humiliated, and nailed on a cross where He struggled to take even a single breath. Jesus knew that all this was necessary, because there was no other way to glorify the Father other than to open the way of Salvation for all who would believe. However, Jesus' sorrow was momentary compared to the inexhaustible joy that was set before Him. People say that the greatest amount of pain is felt by someone giving birth, but joy immediately replaces that pain when the mother sees her newborn child. Jesus died a horrific death. His pain was immense. Yet, that pain passed too after He took His last breath and died. At that moment, He completed the Father's plan and was consumed by the joy of heaven.

Jesus says that the disciples' sorrow will also pass. They *will* see Jesus again. And, when they do, they will be flooded with great joy. While what they dreaded most—being separated from Christ—came to pass, God restored them to Jesus. What joy the disciples must have felt in the presence of the Risen Christ, and nothing could take that feeling away from them. *The key to having joy in the midst of trials is to live in the presence of the Risen Christ.* We can find joy in prison cells like in Rome, on lonely islands like Patmos, and in centers of false religion like Ephesus. If we abide in Christ, the Risen Christ will flood our hearts with heavenly joy that will supersede our circumstances. Don't let the suffering in this world take away your joy both here and the joy that awaits you in heaven. Are you filled with joy?

The Importance of Prayer

In that day you will ask nothing of me. Truly, truly, I say to you,
whatever you ask of the Father in my name, he will give it to you.
Until now you have asked nothing in my name. Ask, and you will
receive, that your joy may be full.

– JOHN 16:23-24

Read Luke 11:1-13

Prayer is an important part of doing the greater works that Jesus said we would do. Immediately after telling His disciples that they would do greater works, Jesus promised that He would do whatever they asked, so that the gospel might be proclaimed to the ends of the earth (John 14:13-14). Then again in John 15, Jesus told His disciples that if they *abide* in Him, they can ask anything, and He will give it to them. Jesus again repeats this promise: "Ask and you will receive." *Throughout this evening, Jesus repeatedly pressed onto His disciples the importance of prayer in spreading the news of the resurrection.* This news was of supreme importance because, through it, the Father would be glorified. Therefore, the Father will mobilize all the resources of heaven to ensure that the gospel goes forth throughout the world.

The disciples had questions about what Jesus meant when He said that in a little while they would not see Him, but in a little while later they would see Him again. They were reticent to ask Jesus and, instead, sought the answer in their own wisdom. The result was frustration at their inability to grasp what Jesus was saying and sorrow at the imminent departure of Jesus. But God doesn't intend to operate through His church in this way. He sent the Spirit to lead us in all truth. If we ask, we will receive an answer. Our prayers will result in the leading of the Spirit in our lives so that we might fulfill the Great Commission.

On several occasions, Jesus taught on the theme, "Ask and you shall receive." After His seminal teaching on prayer

(Luke 11), Jesus immediately told His disciples a parable about a visitor at midnight. The host was under obligation to feed his visitor, but he didn't have any food to offer him. So, he went to his neighbor's house and beseeched the neighbor until he woke up and gave him food. Persevering in prayer resulted in receiving. This is a heavenly principle. God answers *persistent* prayers. And again, Jesus told the parable of the widow who hounded a wicked judge until she received justice (Luke 18:1-8). Her continual asking resulted in her request being granted.

Jesus' point was that if our persistence resulted in an unfriendly heart granting our plea, how much more would the Father who loves us honor our requests to glorify His name by giving us all that we need to further His mission? Jesus explained: "If you then, who are evil, know how to give good gifts to your children, how much more will the heavenly Father give the Holy Spirit to those who ask him" (Luke 11:13)! When we pray and ask only for ourselves, our request is too small. God wants to give us something so much greater. *The ultimate answer to our asking is receiving the Holy Spirit, God's presence in us.* Through our prayers, we ask God to make His glory known among the nations, and to be faithful to go forward to proclaim His salvation to those lost in darkness. Jesus promised that He would be with us *always* as we obeyed the Great Commission. His Spirit is the fulfillment of that promise.

The presence of God, through the Spirit, can turn our sorrow into joy. For the Christ-follower, hardships are a part of our work. However, we are not just co-laborers with Jesus in His mission; we are also His intimate friends. We can ask Him directly, and He will answer us. It's the Spirit who will comfort our hearts in times of hardship. "For as we share abundantly in Christ's sufferings, so through Christ we share abundantly in comfort too" (II Cor. 1:5). Learn to walk in Christ through prayer, bringing your sorrow to Him. As you do, He will turn it into joy. What are you asking the Father to do through you?

The Word and Prayer

I have said these things to you in figures of speech. The hour is coming when I will no longer speak to you in figures of speech but will tell you plainly about the Father. In that day you will ask in my name, and I do not say to you that I will ask the Father on your behalf; for the Father himself loves you, because you have loved me and have believed that I came from God.

— JOHN 16:25-27

Read Colossians 1:9-23

To accomplish the works that Jesus wants us to do means we will need to obey His Word and walk with Him in fellowship through prayer. Once Jesus rises from the dead, and the Spirit is given on the Day of Pentecost, all believers will understand His Word and communicate to God through prayer. After the resurrection, Jesus appeared to His followers on the road to Emmaus, "and beginning with Moses and all the Prophets, he interpreted to them in all the Scriptures the things concerning himself" (Luke 24:27). Jesus took these followers through God's plan of redemption as expressed through Moses and the Prophets so that they would understand that the Messiah had to die and rise again. No longer were the mysteries of the kingdom of God hidden from Jesus' disciples. They were to know God's Word so that they would be able to obey it fully. Likewise, the gospel that we bring to the world is not one that is misunderstood or misinterpreted. Jesus continues to instruct His disciples through the Word.

It's not only the full understanding of the Word that Jesus is giving to us; He's also giving us the authority to ask the Father to glorify Himself through our witness. This is an incredible privilege. As disciples, we no longer need to ask Jesus to intercede for us. We can now ask the Father directly. When we pray, we can approach the Father based on Christ's authority. The Father gave all authority to Christ at His resurrection (Matt. 28:18), therefore we can bring our requests to the Father, and He will answer us.

We can understand God's Word, and know that our requests will be answered not because of our righteousness, but because of our faith in Christ. We are no longer enemies of God. Now, we have become His children. Think about it: children always have access to their father not because of their goodness, but because of their relationship with their father, and because their father loves them. *Christ's death did not just end the hostility between God and us, but fully reconciled our relationship to Him.* We can fully experience the Father's love for us.

This reconciled relationship with God is the strength of our proclamation. When we have trials because of our faith and testimony, we can know that God will actively defend us. For example, a boss may decide that an employee is expendable, a sultan may decide that a slave can be traded, but a father is always protecting his children. In the same way, our heavenly Father is sending us out into a hostile world to bear witness, yet He is also with us. In the midst of our sorrows, we can remember that our Father *loves* us and is working for us.

Through the power of the Holy Spirit, God has given us His presence. He has also given us the tools to access His resources in times of difficulty. When trials come, we need to spend more time in His Word because it is a lamp for our way. God's Word will show us how to walk so that we will not fall into the snares of our enemies. Prayer is also important. Jesus spent long periods in prayer so that He would be faithful to do all that the Father had assigned Him. As we fellowship with God, we too will receive His wisdom to respond to trials as they arise, and we will receive boldness as we proclaim the Good News. The importance of the Word and prayer are evident throughout Jesus' life and instructions to His disciples. They are the ways we abide in Christ and do even His greater works. Are you diligently studying the Word and praying?

The Completed Work of Salvation

I came from the Father and have come into the world, and now I am leaving the world and going to the Father.

– JOHN 16:28

Read John 1:1-18

In this single sentence, Jesus summed up His Father's plan of salvation. From heaven to earth and from earth to heaven, Jesus came to pay our debt of sin, then returned to heaven to show that the Father accepted that payment. This mission was the focus of Jesus' work. He knew what He was going to do, and He focused on that task. Jesus didn't get entangled with the things of the world; He was single minded in His mission.

Jesus said that He came from the Father. This points to Jesus' eternal nature. The Apostle John writes, "In the beginning was the Word, and the Word was with God, and the Word was God" (John 1:1). Jesus is the Word through which all things were created, and His origin is from heaven. *This is important because only an infinitely holy God could pay the massive debt of sin for all believers. It's only heaven that has the capacity to solve this sin problem.* Nothing on earth could ever do it, so the Father acted by sending the Son.

Jesus said that He had come into the world. He was not created. In the incarnation, the eternal Word took on human form. "And the Word became flesh and dwelt among us, and we have seen his glory, glory as of the only Son from the Father, full of grace and truth" (John 1:14). The Son entered time and space hidden behind a veil of humanity. His incarnation was necessary in order that He might fulfill the Law of God. In all of history, only the Son of God was able to fulfill the entire Law. This qualified Jesus to be a sacrifice for our sins, since He didn't die for His own sins. Only Jesus lived a sinless life.

Jesus told his disciples of His coming departure in the last days of His ministry. He told them that He would leave this world through death on a cross. The sinless, perfect Jesus died as a sacrifice for us. He willingly went to the Cross to make a way for our salvation. His sacrifice meant that all of our debt was laid on Jesus as He voluntarily submitted to the Father's will. From the Cross, He proclaimed: "It is finished." The work of Christ was completed. When Jesus died, the sacrifice was made, and the way of salvation was open to all those who would believe.

Finally, it came time for Jesus to go back to the Father. As we've seen, Jesus came from the Father and then returned to the Father. This points to the resurrection and the ascension of Jesus. When Jesus died, our problem of sin was dealt with once and for all, but we would never know that the Father accepted this payment had Jesus not rose from the dead. By taking on all the punishment for our sin, He bore the brunt of the Father's wrath, but death could not defeat Him. And, because He was perfectly holy, Jesus was not consumed by the Father's wrath. *The resurrection was a sign to the world that He was victorious. Now, we can have complete confidence in the fact that the Father accepted Jesus' payment, therefore our sins have been forgiven.* Without the resurrection, we could have never proven that reality on this side of heaven.

Salvation doesn't depend on us. It was God who made the way! He has solved the problem of death and our separation from Him. That work is complete. There is now no need for another incarnation or crucifixion—once and for all, the way of salvation has been secured. If we receive Jesus, we are no longer sinners, but are children of God. The gospel is the only hope for the world; there is no other way. Now that the work of salvation is complete, we can focus on the greater work of proclaiming that salvation to the ends of the earth. Who will you proclaim the gospel to today?

The Proud Heart

His disciples said, "Ah, now you are speaking plainly and not using figurative speech! Now we know that you know all things and do not need anyone to question you; this is why we believe that you came from God."

– JOHN 16:29-30

Read Luke 18:9-17

The Upper Room discourse of Jesus in John 13-17 is packed full of deep truths that require a lot of time to think and pray through in order to understand the truths. There were no short-cuts in learning who Jesus was and what His mission was about. That's why the Holy Spirit was given to the disciples. Without the Spirit, no disciple would be able to fully understand the truths about Jesus. It appeared that the more Jesus taught, the more uneasy the disciples became, but they didn't want to seem as though they didn't understand what Jesus was telling them. Here we see them proudly saying, "At last. Now we got it!" Was this really the great turning point in the disciples' understanding? Jesus knew it wasn't possible without the Spirit, which hadn't yet been given. His disciples were only giving the *appearance* of understanding, when in reality they were confused.

The disciples' statement here echoes many of the proud pronouncements of Peter. If you remember, Peter's pride was on display for all to see on many occasions throughout the gospels. *Pride continues to be an obstacle, preventing us from being shaped into Christ's image and being used by God to spread the gospel.* Perhaps the most important quality of a disciple is humility. Humility starts with the understanding of the gospel. It says that there is nothing that I can do to save myself; God did it all. It says the Father sent the Son, and the Son paid our debt of sin. It was pride that led to our fall into sin through Adam and Eve in the first place, but humility opens us up to receive the salvation that was won for us through Christ. It admits that we were in a hopeless position because of our sin, yet Jesus made a way for us to come back to the Father. Accepting the gospel always takes an attitude of humility, and abiding in Christ requires us to have on-going humility. It's pride that raises obstacles for us to bear fruit for Christ, because our pride tempts us to steal the glory of God for ourselves.

The disciples should have humbled themselves before Christ and said: "We believe. Help our unbelief." Jesus already knew the questions in their minds. He knew their doubts. In place of humility, the disciples became proud because they didn't want to appear weak and ignorant. Peter was famous for covering up his own inadequacies with audacious pronouncements. His attitude spread to the other disciples as well. They, too, were hiding their inadequacies from one another and the Lord. That's what sin does: it hides. After the Fall, Adam and Eve hid from God in the Garden of Eden; they covered up their nakedness with leaves. While we may not be physically hiding from God, we can try to cover-up our sin with leaves of self-righteousness and pride. We can hide our mistakes from others, diverting our responsibility.

A true disciple is one that knows his sin is forgiven, and based on that forgiveness, they will humble themselves before others and God. They don't blame others or their situation for the sins that they commit. *They take full responsibility for their sins and confess them to God and to one another. In doing so, they are proclaiming the gospel.* They are saying that it is not because of *my* self-righteousness that I am restored to the Father, but rather because God replaced my leaves of self-righteousness with the clothes of holiness through the sacrifice of the Lamb of God. God is always glorified when we confess our sins and declare that the gospel is enough. What sins do you need to confess to God today?

God Is with Us Always

Jesus answered them, "Do you now believe? Behold, the hour is coming, indeed it has come, when you will be scattered, each to his own home, and will leave me alone. Yet I am not alone, for the Father is with me."

– JOHN 16:31-32

Read II Timothy 4:9-18

Pride blinds us to reality. It's our proud hearts that can so easily deceive us into a false evaluation of ourselves, because we think more highly of ourselves than we should. Pride causes us to put confidence in ourselves to produce something rather than remembering that our fruit-bearing comes from abiding in Christ. Here, the disciples are in a precarious position. They think they have Jesus all figured out when, in fact, there is so much they have not yet understood. Soon Jesus will die and rise again. Finally, the disciples will know who Jesus truly is: the Son of God.

Jesus exposed the disciples' pride—a pride that set them up to fall. Previously, He confronted Peter after his bold declaration that he would follow Jesus even though all the others deserted Him. Jesus ends up rebuking the disciples, telling them that they should be humble in their faith. The disciples' belief is met head-on by an expression of doubt by Jesus: "Do you really believe?" Even though the disciples had faith, their faith was incomplete. They had confessed Jesus as the Messiah (John 1:41), but they had not yet understood that He was God (John 20:28). *We, too, can become proud in our incomplete understanding of Jesus that we fail to recognize Who He truly is.* Our pride blinds our minds to the truth about Jesus and about ourselves.

Jesus moved quickly to reveal the disciples' incomplete faith. He challenged them by telling them that they don't truly understand who He is and what His mission is. The proof is the disciples' response once Jesus was arrested: they scattered. *In their moment of distress, their faith became paralyzed because it was not rooted in Jesus as Lord.* A follower of Jesus must be ready to die for Christ. If your faith is rooted in a Jesus who is merely a political Savior, you won't be able to withstand the storms that arise when the political power turns against you. However, if your faith is in the Lord Jesus, then whatever Satan throws at you won't matter, because your faith will not falter. You will understand that in the same way Jesus laid down His life for you, you too will lay down your life for Him.

So, instead of fleeing, we can stand firm because the Risen Christ is our defender. Even in the depths of His suffering, Jesus confidently endured the ordeal because He knew that the Father would stay by the Son. The same is true of the Apostle Paul. Christians were increasingly being persecuted by the Roman government. Consequently, Paul was imprisoned in Rome awaiting his execution. Many Christians became ashamed of the gospel and denied it altogether in order to save their lives. In spite of the many Christians who deserted him, Paul knew, even in this inhumane prison, that he was not alone. Paul wrote: "At my first defense no one came to stand by me, but all deserted me... But the Lord stood by me and strengthened me, so that through me the message might be fully proclaimed and all the Gentiles might hear it" (II Tim. 4:16-17).

Both Jesus and the Apostle Paul teach us an important lesson: *The Father doesn't desert the gospel messenger even in the worst of circumstances.* Paul's only concern was that the gospel might fully be proclaimed. He was not concerned about his safety. He knew that God is faithful to His promises to us. We are commissioned to go out into to the world and proclaim the gospel, and, as we do so, He promises to be with us *always*. Even in the worst of situations, God will never leave us. In times of trials, don't rely on your own ideas of who Jesus is. Instead, put your hope in the living Christ as revealed in the Scriptures. *Believe* His promise that He will *never* leave you. Will you stand firm?

Victorious in Christ

I have said these things to you, that in me you may have peace. In the world you will have tribulation. But take heart; I have overcome the world.

– JOHN 16:33

Read I John 2:15-17

After concluding His teaching with a summary of His mission, Jesus encouraged His disciples. Followers of Jesus can expect to have trials in this world. After all, the world is against Christ so it is against us. Satan will use all that is in his arsenal to oppose us, so that the gospel does not spread. Jesus states the obvious. As long as we are still in this world, we can expect trials and tribulations. It's amazing that in light of Jesus' clear teaching on suffering, the church teaches very little on persecution. Some people believe that if we speak about persecution, many disciples will turn back and not stay the course. Believing in Jesus doesn't mean you will have no more problems. It's because you believe in Jesus, that the world will fight against you, but Jesus is *always* with you and is victorious.

We don't have the strength to oppose the world ourselves. When Jesus was arrested, the disciples were filled with fear and fled. They ran away at the first sign of opposition. Why did they do that? They forgot that Jesus had overcome the world. *We can stand firm in our tribulations, not because of our strength, but because of the completed work of Christ on the Cross.* Satan, death, and sin have been defeated forever. Satan tried to tempt Jesus not to fulfill the Father's plan by dying on the Cross. Jesus, however, obeyed the Father and, in so doing, overcame the world. This victory was shared with Jesus' disciples. And although He had not yet died on the cross, He knew that He would not fail in His mission.

The reality of our mission is this: The world will oppose you, but Jesus is victorious. "The light shines in the darkness, and the darkness has not overcome it" (John 1:5). The power of hell cannot prevail over the gospel. Jesus has taken His rightful place on His heavenly throne and will continue to reign throughout all eternity. So, let's get out there and start witnessing! Jesus has given us a task to do and has given us everything we need to do it. It has been over 2,000 years, and the task has not been completed yet; so, strengthen your resolve to proclaim the gospel.

Jesus glorified the Father by doing His work; so too do we glorify God by doing the works that Jesus did. We can only carry out Jesus' mission by abiding in Christ, and we will only produce fruit, despite the opposition we face, when His life flows through us. Thus, take your eyes off of the opposition and look to God; you will only overcome the difficulties through Him. We will do even greater works not because of our training or knowledge, but because Jesus is working on our behalf, through the Spirit. This truth should be a great encouragement to us.

Although the storms rage around us, and we can expect much suffering in the days to come, we can have peace—a peace not found in the world. The world will deceive us by giving an appearance of peace through prosperity, but true peace is a gift that Jesus gives to His followers. This peace is possible as we humble ourselves before God and willingly put to death our selfish desires. When we are consumed by a passion for God's glory, we will boldly face all that the world throws our way, because we are convinced that the peace of Christ is greater than the tribulations of this world. Jesus slept in the middle of the storm. Paul and Silas worshiped in prison. Peter and John calmly testified before the Jewish religious leaders. In these situations, they experienced a supernatural peace. Peace is not the absence of problems; it's knowing that you're securely held in the hands of Jesus. Nothing—pain, imprisonment, loss of reputation, heartache—nothing can ever take us from His hands. We are secure for all of eternity! Are you facing trials with confidence?

The Savior's Prayer

When Jesus had spoken these words, he lifted up his eyes to heaven,
and said, "Father, the hour has come; glorify your Son that the Son
may glorify you"

– JOHN 17:1

Read Matthew 6:5-15

The hour had come. Think about that for a moment. How would you have felt? Jesus knows that the countdown has reached zero. This is the whole reason He came. Although the path before Him was leading to the Cross, He knows that on the other side glory awaits. Jesus kept one mission always before Him: Committing Himself to the Father, knowing that the Father would be glorified by glorifying the Son. So, at this crucial moment, Jesus turned to prayer.

Prayer is an essential part of doing the greater works that Jesus wants us to do. As we've seen, without Christ working through us, we can't produce fruit. Prayer connects us to Christ through dependency, because we acknowledge that apart from Him we can do nothing. Remember, during the course of the night, Jesus repeatedly told His disciples to ask and it will be done for them. Today these verses are often pulled out of context by those naming and claiming material blessings in Jesus' name. Jesus challenges us to boldly pray so that the greater works will happen through us. Not only did Jesus command His disciples to pray, He now gave them an example of a prayer that they should pray. Jesus prayed that the Father's plan of salvation would be fulfilled.

In light of Jesus' command for us to "ask so that it will be done on earth as it is in heaven," it's crucial to look at what Jesus prayed. He prayed that the Father would be glorified through the Son. Even though Jesus knew that the Cross awaited Him, and that soon He would be humiliated, scorned, and subjected to excruciating torture and death, He didn't pray for these things to be lessened. Instead, He prayed that the Father would be glorified. And how was the Father to be glorified? It's through the Son's fulfillment of the Father's plan of salvation. Jesus' utmost concern was always for His Father's glory. And the Father is glorified through the repentance of lost souls. This is a principle that Jesus has consistently taught. In the Lord's Prayer, He taught that we are to first pray that the Father's Name be made holy and that His kingdom will come. This happens when rebellious men and women turn from their sins and worship God. It's only after we pray for the implementation of the Father's plan of salvation, that we turn our attention to our physical needs. *There is nothing greater to be prayed for than the Father's glory.* This should be the most important thing you bring in prayer to the heavenly throne of God.

Jesus not only taught us about prayer, He modeled it. It was Jesus' regular practice to go away and spend time alone with the Father, because He longed for the intimate fellowship with the Father. That made His prayer life so powerful. As a husband longs to hear his wife's voice, so too the Son longed to hear His Father's voice. The Father had given Jesus a difficult, yet crucial task: bearing the sins of the world on the Cross. It was a crushing task. Without complete surrender to the Father, the Son would not have been able to go through with it. Even in Gethsemane, Jesus repeatedly asked for this cup of suffering to be taken from Him. Once again, however, we see that *Jesus is victorious because He brought the weight of this task before the Father in prayer.* If the Son of God needed to continually pray to the Father so that He might faithfully fulfill the Father's will, how much more do we? You can come before the throne of God any time and in any place, asking the Father to glorify His name through you, as you reach souls. You can ask Him to do even greater works through you. And you can pray with complete confidence, knowing that He will always answer your prayer. Have you developed the discipline of prayer?

Jesus' Mission

...since you have given him authority over all flesh, to give eternal life to all whom you have given him. And this is eternal life, that they know you the only true God, and Jesus Christ whom you have sent.

– JOHN 17:2-3

Read John 3:16-21

The Father desires to receive glory, and it is the Son who came to glorify the Father by submitting to His will and dying on the Cross for our sins. This opened the doors of heaven for all who would believe in the Son. *The glory of the Father is linked to giving us eternal life.* Jesus' obedience to the Father should be considered in light of Adam's disobedience. When Adam and Eve sinned in Paradise by disobeying God's command and eating fruit from the forbidden tree, they were attempting to steal God's glory for themselves. They didn't want to glorify God; they wanted to become like God. Humanity still continues to live in rebellion against God today and sets themselves up as gods. We continue to steal the glory that should be directed to God. However, when we confess our sin and humble ourselves before God, saying that we are not God, we give God the glory back.

Jesus' mission is fully connected with giving salvation to the world. When people repent and are given eternal life, glory is given to the Father. It was through the Word that all things were created. Then death entered Creation because of Adam and Eve's sin, but Jesus came to defeat death. He came to give eternal life to all who believe. In so doing, Jesus does what no king, philosophical system, religion, or scientific idea could do. He solved the problem of sin once and for all. By defeating Satan, sin, and death, we can now have eternal life. Jesus is most greatly praised because He did what no one or no system could do. And that is why we see Him worshipped in Heaven as the Lamb that was slain: "Worthy is the Lamb who was slain, to receive power and wealth and wisdom and might and honor and glory and blessing" (Rev. 5:12)!

Only the true God can give us eternal life. No other religion is capable of guaranteeing eternal life. Most religions claim to be the only true religion that worships the only true God; however, they don't have any proof to support their claims. The adherents of these religions will one day face the true God and realize that they blindly followed gods of their own minds. Christianity is different. Christ *did* rise from the dead and is the living God. If you take the founder out of most religions, those religions essentially remain intact. You will still have their rituals, teachings, and beliefs. But if you take Christ out of Christianity, you have nothing. Christianity is not a religion based on rules and traditions, it's a relationship with the living God through Christ. That is why if we are not abiding in Christ, we don't have eternal life.

Jesus is clear on a very important matter: Eternal life is only given to those who *believe* in Christ, because there is no other way to have life or reach God. This truth should make us all the more passionate about proclaiming the gospel. All other religions, except for Christianity, offer salvation on the basis of what *we* do, so if we don't pray or give the right offerings, our debt of sins will not be paid. Christianity is different. The gospel says that you can never pay your debt of sin. In fact, in spite of all your efforts to pay your debt, that debt continues to get larger. The Good News, however, is that *Jesus* paid our debt in full—and He saves us so that God will get all the glory. Are you passionate to proclaim the gospel to all people?

Paid in Full

I glorified you on earth, having accomplished the work that you gave me to do. And now, Father, glorify me in your own presence with the glory that I had with you before the world existed.

– JOHN 17:4-5

Read Luke 9:18-36

Throughout the pages of the Bible, we find the theme of God's glory. Humanity's rebellion against God was a rebellion to usurp God's glory and position. From the beginning, the heavens have proclaimed the glory of God. Satan was cast out of heaven because He wanted to take God's place (Isa.14:12-14). He didn't want to be the creature who must submit to the Creator. In the same way, Satan tempted Adam and Eve telling them to eat the forbidden fruit so that they would become like God. God overcame the wickedness of Satan and the sin of Adam and Eve in a way that resulted in even greater glory for God's name, and as a result, He deserves to be praised.

The glory of God is an important theme in the Bible. God revealed His glory to Israel in the Exodus. Moses, who God raised up, prayed to God on Mount Sinai: "Show me your glory." This glory filled the Temple that Solomon built. As a result of Israel's sin, this glory departed from the Temple and the Jews were expelled from the land of Israel. However, God's plan never fails. The glory of God once again appeared in Jesus Christ. The Apostle John wrote: "And the Word became flesh and dwelt among us, and we have seen his glory, glory as of the only Son from the Father, full of grace and truth" (John 1:14). Jesus Christ is the glory of God in a physical body. He showed that glory to a few of His disciples when He peeled back the veil that covered that glory, "and he was transfigured before them, and his face shone like the sun, and his clothes became white as light" (Matt. 17:2). Elijah and Moses spoke to Jesus about all that

He would accomplish in Jerusalem: He would accomplish our salvation through His death. Therefore, we can see that God's glory is directly connected to the work of salvation performed by Jesus in Jerusalem.

Salvation is God glorifying Himself by solving our greatest problem: we are sinners who can't be in the presence of a holy God. When Isaiah found Himself in God's throne room, the angels proclaimed: "Holy, holy, holy is the Lord of hosts; the whole earth is full of his glory" (Isa. 6:3). Glory is holiness on display. As creatures, we should give the Creator the glory due His name, but because of our sin, we can't be in His holy presence. Praise God that the sin which separates us is now dealt with through Christ's sacrifice, so we can be in His holy presence. In John 1:14, we read that God's glory is full of grace and truth. Without God's grace, we could never glorify His name. Without truth, our praise would be false worship. *In Christ,* this problem is completely resolved. Only Jesus could pay our debt before God and allow us to worship in truth. That's why Jesus is the Way, the Truth, and the Life.

Jesus completed the work of salvation by fulfilling the Father's plan of salvation. The work is done! Jesus bore our sins in His body on the Cross, and His death, resurrection, and ascension have solved humanity's greatest problem—sin and eternal separation from God. That's why Jesus said from the Cross, "It is finished" (John 19:30). When Jesus ascended to heaven, He sat down again on His eternal throne, and returned to heaven to even greater glory. Jesus had taken the form of a lowly servant in order to pay our debt of sin. By surrendering Himself to the Father, He glorified the Father, and His return to heaven meant additional glory. He is the Lord Jesus Christ who, through His earthly life of obedience, is now worshipped throughout eternity. Are you giving glory to Jesus for redeeming us?

Choosing to Obey

I have manifested your name to the people whom you gave me out of the world. Yours they were, and you gave them to me, and they have kept your word.

– JOHN 17:6

Read I Kings 19:19-21

Jesus prayed for His disciples. He knew that the success of their work was not based on their own skills and abilities, but in abiding in Christ. Many people are very intelligent and gifted. Yet they don't produce a harvest of souls for the kingdom of God. God's work of salvation is a *spiritual* work. We are not asking someone to join our club or change their religion. We are introducing them to the Lord Jesus Christ in whom their souls can find peace through the forgiveness of their sins. This is a spiritual ministry that must rely solely on God's power to work in and through us.

Now that Jesus' work was completed, He passed on the next stage of the Father's plan of salvation to His disciples. These disciples were not anything special; they were just normal people with ordinary jobs when Jesus called them. And throughout their training with Jesus, they continually failed to rise to the task. But Jesus was completely at peace as He prayed for those who would continue His work. He knew that the Father had given the disciples to Him, and that the Father knew them and chose them. The Father gave them to the Son for the express purpose of continuing the work of Christ. The Father picked them and gave them to the Son to be trained for the task of proclaiming the gospel. These were handpicked men.

Yet the disciples had a choice to make; they were not mere pawns. They either had to deny themselves and humbly obey God's Word, or they had to live for themselves and miss out on the calling of God. Apart from Judas, they all chose to obey Christ and His Word—the most important choice. God has a calling on each of our lives too, but we have a choice. Unless we are willing to deny ourselves, we won't bear much fruit. Jesus told His disciples that they would bear much fruit if they abided in Christ, through obedience to His Word (John 15:7). The Great Commission is a command that Christ gave His disciples. Obedience is required. In the same way that the disciples were sent, so too are we sent out to make disciples of all nations. This means putting aside our selfish interests for God's interests. We now take on a new ambition: to glorify His name by bringing many to faith in Christ.

In the history of salvation, God has repeatedly chosen people of every age to obey Him, by choosing to do His work of salvation over their own agendas. For example, Noah chose to obey God by building the Ark. Abraham obeyed by leaving Ur, and heading to a destination that would be revealed later. Moses chose to identify with God's people rather than the riches of Egypt. None of these men were sinless, nor did they obey perfectly, but their lives were characterized by *choosing God* over themselves and the world. In the same way, we must make our choice. When I was in the university, I knew that God was calling me to proclaim the gospel. However, I was also smart and had a promising career ahead of me. At that moment, I was confronted with a choice: Would I obey God's plan for my life or would I choose to live for myself? I chose God's plan, but it was challenging. As disciples, every one of us has to examine our lives. Bearing fruit is contingent on abiding in Christ, and abiding is contingent on obeying Christ. We need to reaffirm our commitment to Christ to fulfill His calling on our lives. Will you choose to do God's will and place His glory above your own?

Faith in Christ

Now they know that everything that you have given me is from you.
For I have given them the words that you gave me, and they have
received them and have come to know in truth that I came from you;
and they have believed that you sent me.

– JOHN 17:7-8

Read John 6:44-71

Throughout the pages of the gospel, we can't help but be struck by the disciples' lack of faith. In the Gospel of Matthew, for example, Jesus repeatedly says to His disciples: "You have little faith." Now that Jesus will soon be departing, the question of the strength of the disciples' faith becomes critical. Will they have enough faith in Christ to accomplish His work? Jesus doesn't waver on the answer to this important question. He knows that they do because "they have believed that you sent me." Here is the important principle that we so desperately need to understand: *The key is not in the strength of our faith, but rather in the* object *of our faith.* If we have faith that Jesus is the Son of God sent to fulfill the Father's plan of salvation, then we have enough faith to do the greater works that Jesus promised we would do. Every believer whose faith is in Christ can do it, because abiding in Christ is about being in the True Vine, so His life can flow through us and produce fruit.

Jesus gives us a positive statement about the disciples' faith. This might seem misguided since, in a few moments when Jesus is arrested in Gethsemane, His disciples will all flee out of fear, leaving Jesus to face the Cross alone. Their faith is certainly not complete. They still don't understand the resurrection that will take place in a few days. But the disciples have reached a decisive point in their relationship with Christ here. When Jesus first appeared on the scene, many were drawn to Him because of the miraculous healings and the feeding of thousands. People followed

Jesus in hopes that He would fulfill their needs. However, as the miracles decreased in frequency, and, as they understood that Jesus was not going to lead a rebellion against the Roman occupiers, the Jews turned on Him. More and more people deserted Jesus and asked for Him to be crucified. In spite of their weak faith, the disciples stayed, because they understood that Jesus was different. They didn't depart even when they heard the difficult truths that Jesus taught. They were even willing to lay down their lives for Him (John 13:37). You could look closely at their faith and certainly conclude that their faith wasn't strong, but it was directed in the right object—Jesus Christ as revealed by the Father.

The world is constantly trying to remake Jesus according to what they want. The Jews wanted a political Messiah that would lead a rebellion. Today, some want a Jesus who will give us whatever we ask, so that our lives will be materially blessed. Others still want a Jesus who is a good moral teacher. A disciple is a person who doesn't define Jesus according to what they want or feel is true. A disciple is someone who accepts that the words that Jesus spoke are directly from the Father and are true. It's believing in the Jesus revealed by the Father and not the Jesus of our own understanding. Only the Jesus revealed by the Father can solve our greatest problem: sin. By humbling ourselves and accepting who Jesus is, we'll stop trying to make a Jesus of our liking.

The disciples eventually had such faith. Even though their courage failed them on occasions like in the Garden of Gethsemane, they didn't waver in their view of Jesus: Jesus is the Son who came to fulfill the Father's plan of salvation. Now, like the disciples, we have to choose to obey God's Word and put our faith in Jesus just as the Father has revealed Him to us. We need to accept that this Jesus is enough. As we abide in Him, our faith will increase and become stronger. Are you believing the revealed Jesus or a Jesus of your own understanding?

Jesus Prays for Us

I am praying for them. I am not praying for the world but for those
whom you have given me, for they are yours. All mine are yours, and
yours are mine, and I am glorified in them.

— JOHN 17:9-10

Read Hebrews 7:20-28

Jesus knew the importance of prayer. In fact, prayer was a regular practice of our Lord. He prayed first to the Father, then He prayed for His disciples, and after that He prayed for the world. Our spiritual lives should also reflect this same pattern. We need to spend personal prayer time with God, asking Him to draw us nearer to Himself. It's in our prayer times, that He shows us what needs to be pruned in our lives so we will bear even more fruit. It's the Holy Spirit's job to reveal the sins in our lives that need to be confessed. As we fellowship with the Father through prayer, we will also better understand our calling and the Father's heart for making His glory known to the ends of the earth.

Followers of Jesus need to be prayed for as well. We should pray for our brothers and sisters in Christ, who have committed to doing the greater works that Jesus wants us to do. If we are to bear much fruit, we need to be bathed in prayer. *What do we pray?* We pray for unity among the disciples, protection as they proclaim the Good News, and that they will set themselves apart to fulfill God's mission. Then we pray that the world will open their eyes to the truth about Christ and worship Him as their Savior and Lord.

Disciples of Jesus are truly blessed. Even in times of great trials and difficulties, we can *know* that Jesus and the Holy Spirit are both interceding for us to the Father. The Apostle Paul tells us that even when we don't know how to pray, "the Spirit intercedes for the saints according to the will of God" (Rom. 8:27). When we are abiding in Christ and doing His work, the Spirit is taking the cries of our hearts, translating them into God's will, and bringing them before the Father. That's why all things work together for our good (Rom. 8:28). When we have denied ourselves and obeyed the Word of Christ by proclaiming the Good News, *God works on our behalf to fulfill our heart's desire to glorify His name in the midst of our trials.* It is not only the Spirit who is interceding on our behalf; the Son, as our eternal High Priest, is also interceding also for us in heaven (Heb. 7:25). Jesus is still active in Heaven praying for us just as He prayed for His twelve disciples.

Our unity, personal holiness, and boldness are a fruit of divine intercession, and we are strengthened by God to do the work that Christ did, because His ability to keep and sustain us testifies to the oneness of the Father and Son. Our relationship to the Father and the Son reflects this truth. The Father as the vinedresser, and the Son as the vine, are both concerned about the branches. The Father prunes the branches, and the Son gives life to the branches. Together, they work in unison so that we will produce fruit. As we do the work that Christ did, we are revealing to the world that the Father and the Son are one. We pray to the Father in the name of the Son, and we abide in Christ to do the Father's will. The Father, Son, and Spirit all work together to glorify God through the redemption of sinners. How does the knowledge that Jesus and the Holy Spirit are interceding for you impact your life and ministry?

Safe and Secure

And I am no longer in the world, but they are in the world, and I am coming to you. Holy Father, keep them in your name, which you have given me, that they may be one, even as we are one. While I was with them, I kept them in your name, which you have given me. I have guarded them, and not one of them has been lost except the son of destruction, that the Scripture might be fulfilled.

– JOHN 17:11-12

Read Romans 8:29-39

Satan has been actively working to thwart God's plan of redemption at every turn. After Satan was expelled from heaven, he committed himself to destroying humankind who were made in God's image. Satan tempted Adam and Eve, so that they disobeyed God and sinned. And from that point onward, Satan has attacked every stage of God's plan. Events such as the Flood, the sins of the Patriarchs, Israel's disobedience in the wilderness, the pollution of Temple worship, and the rejection of the Messiah were all efforts by Satan to undermine God's plan. Satan worked extra hard to attack Jesus. When Jesus was born, he stirred up King Herod to kill all the young boys his age. He also tempted Jesus in the wilderness so that Jesus would worship Satan and not go to the Cross. Even in the Garden of Gethsemane, Satan was there as Jesus prayed with tears of blood streaming down His face—but Jesus was victorious.

Now, Satan has turned His attention to us. Since he was not successful in thwarting God's plan of salvation, he is now trying to keep us from spreading salvation to those in bondage to Satan. Satan is actively at work against us. He is called our adversary and is looking to destroy us. While Jesus was on earth, He protected His disciples. For example, they were safe in spite of the storms that fell on them as they sailed across the Sea of Galilee. Although they would experience weariness and struggles in ministry, they were safe from the Devil's schemes, because they were in Jesus' care. Even when Jesus was arrested, He protected His disciples so that none of them were arrested. Only Jesus was put on trial and crucified, because Jesus kept His disciples safe so that they could bear witness to the resurrection.

Jesus is still protecting us through His intercession for us. Although Jesus is no longer physically present as He was with His disciples, He is involved in our situations through His prayers. *His prayers for our protection are not so we can have a long and comfortable life but so we remain united as we are experiencing attacks from the Devil.* The Devil knows that physical suffering doesn't hinder the proclamation of the gospel. In spite of the great persecution experienced by the church throughout the ages, the gospel continued to go forward. But in times of prosperity and peace, it's easy to be tempted by the world, rather than obeying Christ. When we are attacked from *without,* it can bring us together. When we are attacked from *within,* it can divide us. Jesus doesn't pray that we will be safe from our enemies; He prays that we will be *one* so that the proclamation of the gospel won't be destroyed by disunity. Our unity not only reflects the spiritual truth of the oneness of the Father and the Son, but it's essential for our witness to the world.

Jesus is still praying for the protection of His disciples, although He knows the power of prayer. His intercession is effective, because His prayers are in accordance with the Father's will. Therefore, we can have great confidence knowing that we are more than conquerors through Christ who gives us strength. Are you one with other disciples?

Filled with Jesus' Joy

But now I am coming to you, and these things I speak in the world,
that they may have my joy fulfilled in themselves.

– JOHN 17:13

Read Hebrews 10:32-39

It might seem strange that on the night of His arrest, and knowing that He would be crucified on the following day, Jesus spoke a lot about having joy. Jesus was filled with joy not because His life was comfortable, but because He was fulfilling the Father's plan. No earthly pain or loss could deny Him of the heavenly joy of knowing that He was doing the Father's will. The world continually offers us pleasure and entertainment as a counterfeit to keep us from choosing heavenly joy. Satan even made that same offer to Jesus, when he offered all the kingdoms of the world to Jesus, if Jesus would bow down and worship him. What an offer! Jesus could have all of earth's pleasures, power, and status and, at the same time, avoid bearing our sins on the Cross. But Jesus knew that all the suffering and hardship of the Cross were nothing compared to the overwhelming joy He would have in heaven. Jesus is our example because "for the joy that was set before him endured the cross, despising the shame, and is seated at the right hand of the throne of God" (Heb. 12:2).

Choosing heavenly joy over earthly pleasures is a mark of spiritual maturity. *As we abide more in Christ, we will grow in maturity, and deny ourselves, choosing heavenly joy over our earthly pleasures.* Jesus again puts this choice before His disciples. He told them that He spoke these things so that their joy might be made full (John 15:11). He promised to answer their prayers so that their gospel witness would not be hindered and that their joy would be fulfilled (John 16:24). Jesus is again speaking of joy. He wants joy to fill His disciples. He is praying that the disciples will choose obedience to the Word of God, rather than choosing the path of accommodation with the world.

Being filled with Jesus' joy is attainable to each and every disciple, but it's only found in rejecting Satan's offer. We must always be aware of Satan's schemes. The Devil is trying to sell us a false, shallow pleasure by calling it joy. Satan is a counterfeiter. In many parts of the world, you can purchase designer purses, watches, etc. I was offered a Rolex watch for $10 once. It worked for three days before it stopped. Counterfeits like this look like the real thing, but they are cheap fakes. Satan continues to offer us cheap counterfeits that look like the original that God wants to give us, without the cost that must be paid to attain it. Jesus could have avoided the Cross, if He bowed down to Satan, but the pleasures that Satan offered Jesus would have soon turned to shame. Now Satan, through the world, is trying to trick us into buying his counterfeit joy, by wrapping it up in materialism and prosperity. Beware of Satan's junk!

Real joy is experienced when sinners repent. The New Testament is filled with declarations of joy. There was joy at the birth of Jesus, because the Savior was born. There is joy when one person finds the gospel (Matt. 13:44). In fact, all of heaven rejoices (Luke 15:10). Jesus was filled with joy because He made a way for sinners to be redeemed. His disciples were filled with joy when they proclaimed the gospel and sinners found redemption. The early church faced persecution with joy, because they knew that the gospel was going out to the people who needed to hear it. The Apostle Paul, in prison, could write with joy, "Rejoice in the Lord always; again I will say rejoice" (Phil. 4:4). Nothing can replace the joy heaven gives to disciples when they do the greater works of proclaiming the gospel and sinners repent. Are you filled with this joy?

Under the Father's Protection

I have given them your word, and the world has hated them because
they are not of the world, just as I am not of the world. I do not ask
that you take them out of the world, but that you keep them from
the evil one. They are not of the world, just as I am not of the world.

– JOHN 17:14-16

Read II Timothy 3:10-17

Often, we think of salvation in terms of what we are
saved *from*; however, we must also consider what we are
saved *for*. The gospel saved us from eternal destruction.
Jesus paid our debt of sin so we can now live forever in
heaven and glorify God. The gospel has also saved us for an
important task. We are called to make disciples (Matt. 28:19-
20), meaning we are to go to those who are not believers yet
and share the gospel with them so that they can join us in
worshipping God. This is the work that Jesus did, and this
is the work that we are commissioned to do as well.
Regardless of the obstacles and the opposition, we must
faithfully do this work.

Satan opposes every disciple that is doing the work of
the gospel. In fact, to be a Christian is to face opposition
from the world. Jesus tells us that the world will hate us
because we don't follow the world's pursuit of pleasure.
Instead, we are to obtain life and joy through denying
ourselves. That's the opposite of what the world is telling
us. Satan despises people who become disciples of Christ,
so he stirs up the world against us, in an attempt to steal our
joy. Choosing joy instead of pleasure is really the equivalent
of choosing Jesus over Satan. Jesus tells us that He is not of
this world; He came to fulfill the Father's plan of salvation.
As we align ourselves with Christ and follow His example
of self-denial, we will show others that we are not of this
world. Instead, our allegiance is to Christ and obeying the
Father's will for our lives.

Knowing that they would face such opposition, Jesus committed to praying for the disciples. However, He didn't pray that they wouldn't experience trials and difficulties. All disciples will share in Christ's suffering as part of being a follower of Christ. *Jesus prayed that they would be protected against the attacks that would surely come as they shared the gospel.* These were the ones that the Father gave to spread the Good News of the resurrection throughout the world. If they were taken out of the world, then there would be no one to testify on Christ's behalf, so Jesus entrusted them to the Father's keeping. This keeping is a ministry of God to every disciple who is witnessing the truth of salvation through Christ. It doesn't mean that there isn't a possibility of martyrdom for followers of Christ. What it means is that in the midst of these trials and difficulties, the Lord will give them the strength to endure to the end.

Some Christians think it's best to protect themselves by forming special communities where they can live separate from the world, but withdrawing from the world is not God's will. Others think they should stand up for their rights and fight back against the world. And still others think that we are best served by working with the world to further social programs that help the needy. Neither isolation, nor confrontation, nor assimilation is God's will for His disciples. Our relationship to the world must be formed by what the Bible describes as the root cause of the world's opposition to God and God's solution for that problem. The world opposes God, because they want to be God. Until sin is dealt with and removed, the world will continue to oppose God and His church. The solution then is proclamation. The gospel is the *only* solution to the world's problems, so we must proclaim it, because God has called us to bear fruit. Faithfully proclaiming the gospel so that His kingdom comes and His will be done on earth as it is being done in heaven, is the mission of every disciple. How are you engaging the world?

Commissioned

Sanctify them in the truth; your word is truth. As you sent me into the world, so I have sent them into the world. And for their sake I consecrate myself, that they also may be sanctified in truth.

— JOHN 17:17-19

Read Romans 12:1-2

The third prayer request that Jesus offered on behalf of His disciples was sanctification. Often, we misinterpret the word 'sanctification' in this verse to mean personal holiness. Sanctification here means to be set apart or separate. *Jesus was asking the Father to set the disciples apart to spread the gospel. Jesus' prayer was really a prayer of commissioning.* Now that Jesus was completing the Father's plan, the torch needed to be passed to the disciples. Jesus' prayer revealed that the disciples' commission was a divine decision born through the Son's prayer to the Father.

Jesus was sanctified or set apart to fulfill the Father's plan of salvation. He was the Lamb of God that took away the sins of the world. In the Temple, unblemished lambs were set apart for sacrifice on the altar. They were to be dedicated and offered to God. Jesus had also prayed consecrating Himself as the Lamb of God. After His death on the Cross, no other lambs would need to be sacrificed. All the sacrificial lambs in the Temple were symbols for the Israelites to remember that God would one day permanently take away their sins. Jesus became our sacrifice on the Cross by submitting to the Father's will and humbling Himself to the point of death.

Because Christ was set apart as our ultimate sacrifice, the disciples were to also be set apart. Our sanctification is different from Jesus' sacrifice. Jesus was the Lamb that was dedicated for sacrifice. The disciples were not dedicated to be a sacrifice for sin. Instead, they were set apart for a special mission. In the Old Testament, God often set apart prophets (Jer. 1:5) and priests (Exo. 40:13; Lev, 8:30) for special purposes. These people no longer lived their lives as they did before. Instead they stopped what they were doing to focus all their energy on their new assignment. For example, Elisha was sanctified or set apart as a prophet when he was out plowing his field. Immediately, he stopped his career as a farmer, sacrificed his oxen, and served the Lord.

Jesus prayed so that His disciples would be set apart by the Father for the task of witnessing to the sacrifice of the Lamb of God. If they isolated themselves from the world, there would be no testimony. If they lived worldly lives, they would not be able to exhibit the power of the gospel and call people to repentance. They needed to be set apart to engage the world with the Good News. By doing so, the gospel would be clearly heard as people were warned of the judgment to come (I Pet. 4:1-6). Therefore, Jesus' disciples and all disciples after them, need to be sanctified in the renewing of their minds. In other words, Christ's disciples need to stop becoming like the world, and abide in Christ instead. As we do so, we will understand His will for our lives and we'll make the changes necessary in our lives to bear fruit for His glory.

We are sanctified by the truth. This truth is not some general principle for living or a code of ethics. It's God's Word or revelation, the revelation that is supremely seen in the Father's plan of salvation. *The truth that sanctifies us is the Cross of Christ.* The Cross reveals the model for doing God's will: Jesus humbled Himself and obediently died on the cross. In the same way, His disciples are to deny themselves and abide in Christ through humility. We are to die to ourselves and the world, and we are to strive to fill the world with God's glory. This mission is what sets us apart. Are you willing to be set apart from the world to fulfill this mission?

The Testimony of Our Unity

I do not ask for these only, but also for those who will believe in me through their word, that they may all be one, just as you, Father, are in me, and I in you, that they also may be in us, so that the world may believe that you have sent me.

– JOHN 17:20-21

Read Romans 15:8-21

The gospel spread through the witness of Jesus' original disciples to people all around the world. Jesus knew that His disciples would bear fruit, and that the Holy Spirit would convict people of their sin when they heard the Good News. He also knew people would come to faith through repentance when they heard about Jesus' death and resurrection. Therefore, Jesus prays for these future believers. Jesus, our High Priest, not only gave Himself as a sacrifice of atonement to pay our debt of sin, but He continues His priestly duties by making intercession for every believer. *Jesus is praying that through our lives, the gospel might go out to everyone.*

Jesus' prayer for all believers is that they might be one. This oneness is not an earthly oneness, but a spiritual one. It reflects the relationship of the Father to the Son. We can only have this unity if we first have the spiritual life of God flowing through us. Oneness is based on being in the vine. Our abiding in Christ means, that just as every branch is one in the vine, so too we are all one in Christ. Becoming part of the vine is accomplished through salvation in Jesus Christ. "But to all who did receive Him, who believed in his name, he gave the right to become children of God" (John 1:12). All believers are one because we are children of one Father. On the Day of Pentecost, the Holy Spirit filled all who believed. In other words, they were spiritually brought into a relationship with Christ.

However, the work of Christ didn't end there. The

disciples obeyed the Great Commission by proclaiming the gospel in other lands. As a result, people from different races also put their faith in Christ. This caused a conflict among the believers from Jewish backgrounds. Their previous religion taught them that they were right and everyone else was wrong, so they were greatly prejudiced towards people who were not Jews. But, soon the gospel message had reached so many non-Jews that the Jewish influence over the church was being lost. The Laws of Moses were being forced on all believers from believers with Jewish backgrounds, but this was not the gospel. The gospel says we are *not* saved by keeping the Law, but through faith in Jesus Christ alone. That's why the Apostle Paul said: "For in one Spirit we were all baptized into one body—Jews or Greeks, slaves or free—and all were made to drink of one Spirit" (I Cor. 12:13).

Our unity with other believers is a testimony to the world, so it's important that we all get along. It shows the world that Jesus Christ is Lord, because people will put aside their prejudices and feelings of superiority to humbly submit to Christ. Not only is the Son the only one who can pay our debt of sin, He is also the only one who can unify humanity, because the Son humbly submitted to the Father. As His disciples humbly submit to Him, the world will know that Jesus is Lord. *Branches in the vine come in all shapes and sizes, but they all have one thing in common: The life of the vine flows through them, causing them to bear fruit.* As we all abide in Christ, the Spirit will work to bear fruit through us. We need to remember that all believers have one Savior and one mission. We can rejoice in our differences knowing that God has created us to serve Him in different places and in different contexts, but always with the same mission: to proclaim to the world that Jesus is Lord. How is your unity with other believers testifying to the gospel?

God's Missionary Strategy

The glory that you have given me I have given to them, that they may be one even as we are one, I in them and you in me, that they may become perfectly one, so that the world may know that you sent me and loved them even as you loved me.

– JOHN 17:22-23

Read I Peter 1:13-25; Galatians 6:14

God desires that all should be saved through faith in Jesus. So, it's interesting that while Jesus prays for Himself, His disciples, and all believers, He doesn't pray for the lost souls of this world. That doesn't mean that Jesus is not concerned about the world. From Scripture, we know that the Father loved the world so much that He sent His Son, Jesus, to save us (John 3:16). Instead of praying for the world, Jesus prays for all believers, because He knows that all who abide in Him will bear fruit by proclaiming salvation to the world. *The most important prayer that can be offered for the world, then, is for believers to proclaim the gospel so that the world will believe in Christ and have eternal life.*

Jesus gave us His glory so that we would be one and, that through that oneness, the world would come to faith in Him. Jesus often spoke of glory and being glorified. This glory referred to His death and resurrection. Jesus said, "The hour has come for the Son of Man to be glorified" (John 12:23). God is most glorified through the fulfillment of His plan of salvation. Jesus went to the Cross to glorify the Father and, was in turn, glorified by the Father. Jesus prayed, "But for this purpose I have come to this hour. Father, glorify your name" (John 12:27-28). The Cross was the ultimate expression of God's glory. In the Cross, God's justice, righteousness, holiness, and love are displayed for all the world to see. The Father poured out His wrath on the Son, so that we would become recipients of His love through grace.

This glory has been given to us so that we might become perfectly one. The glory of the Cross is the Son humbly submitting to the Father's will and denying Himself, even to the point of death on the Cross. Now we, as His disciples, must take up our own cross. In fact, we find glory in the ministry of the Cross. With humility, we can testify to the salvation that Christ has given us and, through self-denial, can give of ourselves so that others might be saved through Christ's sacrifice. We can become perfectly one with other believers, because of our common salvation. We are one in the ministry of the Cross. And as a result, the church throughout the world gives itself fully to the cause of the gospel. Carrying our cross is not burdensome, but rather a privilege. When Jesus fell on the way to Golgotha, Simon the Cyrene, was tasked by the Roman guard to pick up Jesus' cross and carry it the rest of the way for Him. The curse of the Cross was borne by Jesus alone. However, we can carry the cross of salvation with honor, knowing that our obedience brings glory to God. The Apostle Paul writes, "If we are afflicted, it is for your comfort and salvation" (II Cor. 1:6). Our suffering is for the salvation of others.

The missionary strategy of God is that the church—believers filled with the Holy Spirit—will form new communities around the world to exhibit God's love and salvation by what they say and do. As we live in a community modeled on the oneness of the Father and Son, the world will know that Jesus is Lord and Savior, and will come to understand God's great love for them. Before anything else was created, the Father loved the Son. This love is an unceasing perfect love. Jesus says, that through our oneness, the world will know that this love is also for them. Through Jesus, we can have a love relationship with God for all eternity. It's this oneness with God that is a proclamation to the world that God loves them. If God can save people like us, then the world will know that they, too, can be saved—no one is beyond the reach of the work of Christ. Are you exhibiting God's love to the world?

Jesus' Desire

Father, I desire that they also, whom you have given me, may be with me where I am, to see my glory that you have given me because you loved me before the foundation of the world.

– JOHN 17:24

Read I John 1:1-2:6

Everyone wants to be wanted. We all have a longing in our heart to have community and acceptance. We experience this because we are made in God's image, and because God is relational. God is all about relationship and desires to have a relationship with us. This is His heart. He loves us and wants to give us the most pleasurable and fulfilling thing that we could ever desire. He doesn't need to guess at what we need, because He already knows that our deepest longing can only be fulfilled by Himself. We were created to have fellowship with God. That was the greatest blessing that Adam enjoyed. When He fellowshipped with God as God walked with Adam and Eve in the coolness of the day in the garden, what joy must have filled his heart. God was with them and they were with God. However, that fellowship was destroyed by Adam and Eve's sin. Because they didn't obey God, they reaped the consequences of that decision: God would not dwell with sinful people.

However, God in His goodness and love, worked to rectify this problem and restore our fellowship with Himself. The Bible teaches us that the glory of Jesus is the glory of redemption. All the inhabitants of heaven give praise to the Lamb singing, "for you were slain, and by your blood you ransomed people for God from every tribe and language and people and nation" (Rev. 5:9). Christ wants us to be in heaven with Him before the throne, and has provided the way for that to happen. This glory was given because the Father loved the Son. This love was an eternal love arising "before the foundation of the world."

Amazingly, God planned the redemption of sinners through His Son's death and resurrection before Adam and Eve even sinned. He knew what would happen if He created humans. However, He also knew that through their redemption, God would receive the highest glory. Although He was grieved by our sin, He knew that He would make a way to restore this fellowship forever.

Jesus promised His disciples that, although He would depart from them, He was going to prepare a place for them in His Father's house. He would once again come back to take them there (John 14:1-3). Heaven is living with God in His house. The Apostle John describes the New Jerusalem, our eternal abode, as a city made of pure gold with the foundations of the walls adorned with jewels, but living in the most luxurious place imaginable is not our greatest joy. Neither is having eternity in our new bodies or being with our fellow believers. *Our greatest joy is to be in heaven to see Jesus in His glory and to be with Him forever.* John writes that, "the throne of God and of the Lamb will be in it, and his servants will worship him. They will see his face" (Rev. 22:3-4). We will be filled with joy in heaven, because we will finally see Jesus' glory and experience the fullness of His love.

Understanding that God can restore our fellowship with Himself, the greatest desire of our hearts, should change how we live in this world. Jesus has promised that we can *know* that we have eternal life, and that heaven is ours. And because we know that all humans were created for heaven, our hearts should become distressed when we see those who are still living in sin. We should desire that they, too, know God, because God is most glorified by each person that worships Jesus Christ as Lord. The world continues to fill the void in their lives with temporary, material blessings, but none of these things will ever provide the eternal delight that we have in Christ. What a privilege to give ourselves fully to the work of proclaiming the gospel so that many other will join us in heaven! Will you give yourself to that endeavor?

Jesus Knows The Father

*O righteous Father, even though the world does not know you, I
know you, and these know that you have sent me.*

– JOHN 17:25

Read Romans 3:19-28

Every day the media is seemingly filled with reports of
bad news. If you only paid attention to the media, you would
think that nothing good ever happens anywhere in the
world. Bad news sells. People like to hear it and are
fascinated by it. Jesus doesn't end His prayer by trying to
pique the interest of His disciples. His prayer wasn't for
them. Jesus was praying to the Father. The content of this
prayer centered around the gospel message. Jesus knows the
Father is righteous and that the world is lost in sin, and that
it is only the Father who can make a way for the world to
come back to Him. This is the kind of prayer that God
wants from us. The more we understand the glory of God
as expressed through salvation, the more we will pray,
"Your kingdom come, your will be done." We know that
the gospel is the only hope for the world, so we need to
continually ask God to glorify His name by revealing the
truth about Christ to the world.

Sadly, the world doesn't know Christ. Their minds
have been too dulled by sin and their eyes have been blinded
to the truth about Jesus. Paul described the world's spiritual
condition: "In their case the god of this world has blinded
the minds of the unbelievers, to keep them from seeing the
light of the gospel of the glory of Christ, who is the image
of God" (II Cor. 4:4). They are lost in their sin and captives
in Satan's kingdom of darkness. Even if they knew of their
miserable condition, they have no ability in and of
themselves to be set free from Satan.

In spite of the desperate condition of the world, there
is good news: Jesus knows the Father. Jesus is the highest
and most perfect expression of who the Father is. He knows

how much the Father loves even the lost and rebellious. What is the Good News? It is that there is hope for even the worst of sinners. God has taken the initiative to completely resolve the matter of our sin before Him. *Each day as our debt of sin grows, Jesus knows exactly the payment that the Father requires.* Our good works cannot pay this debt. There is no guessing. So, when Jesus proclaimed from the Cross, "It is finished," He could guarantee that the Father's plan for our salvation was completed. *He paid it all.* All. "And you, who were dead in your trespasses and the uncircumcision of your flesh, God made alive together with him, having forgiven us all our trespasses, by canceling the record of debt that stood against us with its legal demands. This he set aside, nailing it to the cross" (Col. 2:13-14). Our debt is paid. We can once again worship God.

Although the world doesn't know the Father, there is a way for the world to know Him again: believing in the Son. This is the definition of a disciple—one who knows the Son. This means that we believe that we are sinners and that Jesus is the divine Son who came to pay our debt of sin. Because of what Jesus did on the Cross, our debt of sin is paid in full. This payment was a great exchange. Jesus took our sins upon Himself and put His righteousness on us. Now when the Father looks at us, He doesn't see our sin; He sees Jesus' perfect righteousness.

The one and only way to solve the problem of sin is Jesus Christ. If we don't know Him, we don't have eternal life. Disciples, who know the Father, will proclaim the Good News. Jesus' righteousness is enough to cover all the sins committed throughout history. Therefore, we need to work diligently to get the news out to others so that they, too, might believe that the Father sent the Son. How has knowing Jesus changed your life?

Continually Abiding

I made known to them your name, and I will continue to make it known, that the love with which you have loved me may be in them, and I in them.

– JOHN 17:26

Read Colossians 1:24-29; Galatians 2:20

The work of salvation is complete. Jesus paid our debt of sin, and salvation is made available to all who believe. Jesus has perfectly revealed the Father to us, so we can come to know God. Jesus will soon depart, and it will be time for the disciples to continue to do the work that Jesus did. Now, it's our turn to act. God entrusted the spreading of salvation to us. Throughout John 13-17, God has promised us that we will bear much fruit as we abide in Him, through humility and self-denial. *Jesus' final statement in His prayer on this night is a prayer of promise.* He promises to continue the work of making the Father's name known. This promise is our hope, and our abiding in Christ is maintained and strengthened through continually growing in understanding the Father through His Word. The more we know the Father, the greater our faith will be, and the greater our obedience to the Father will be.

Jesus' death and resurrection was the greatest revelation of the Father's love and righteousness. Once Jesus returned to the Father, He continues revealing the Father to us, so we are not abandoned in our mission. While Jesus commanded us to proclaim the gospel to all peoples, He also gave us the Spirit, so that we will have the power to fulfill His command. God wants you and I to do great things for Him, because the world needs to hear of the great salvation that God has provided for all who believe. In our struggle for the souls of the lost, we can confidently do the works that Jesus did, because we know that Jesus has promised to continue to work through us to make the

Father known. This is not mission impossible. God has given us all we need to fulfill this mission. Therefore, we can work with all our strength, because we know that the great strength of God is at work through us.

Abiding in Christ is the key to doing the work that Jesus did. The Apostle Paul learned this lesson and practiced it in his ministry. Paul knew that he was weak, and the burden of ministry was overwhelming at times, even to the point where he wished he could die and be with the Lord (II Cor. 1:9). God permitted Satan to torment Paul through a "thorn in his flesh". However, Paul remained strong and faithful and finished his race, because he knew the secret of abiding in Christ—"when I am weak, then I am strong" (II Cor. 12:10). Fruit-bearing is only possible if God does the work through us. That's why Paul encourages Timothy to, "be strengthened by the grace that is in Christ Jesus" (II Tim. 2:1). Only by abiding in Christ and His work of grace, can we proclaim the gospel and bring a harvest of souls to the throne room of heaven. Praise God for His permanent abiding in us: We are His and He is ours.

Christ's words in the Upper Room began, "Now before the Feast of the Passover, when Jesus knew that his hour had come to depart out of this world to the Father, having loved his own who were in the world, he loved them to the end" (John 13:1). The fulfillment of the Father's plan of salvation was a result of Jesus' great love for us. As Jesus ends His prayer, He once again draws our attention to that love. The love that brought Jesus to the Cross is the Father's eternal love for the Son (John 17:24, 26). That love also motivates us to obey the Great Commission by doing the greater works that Jesus has prepared for us. There is no higher privilege than to be called to this task. Give your life, your family, and all your hopes and dreams to this endeavor. May your love for the lost and your desire to glorify God lead you to change the world by bringing many to heaven. Jesus is with you, abide continually in Him, because you have been *appointed to bear fruit*!

Epilogue

We cannot begin to fathom the depth of distress and anguish experienced by Jesus on the night of His arrest. In the midst of this great personal struggle, Jesus took time to teach, comfort, and pray for His disciples. Reflecting on His words in John 13-17, leaves us with an overwhelming sense of awe of Jesus' great sacrifice for us. None of His words of hope or promises of eternal life would mean anything if He wasn't willing to submit to the Father and drink from the cup of suffering, but Jesus *was* willing to pay the price so that others might glorify God.

As we follow Jesus, we too must realize that as disciples, we must be ready to pay a price in order to bear fruit. We haven't been saved to live comfortable lives. Our citizenship is now in heaven. We have a higher calling as Jesus' disciples: God has appointed us to *bear fruit* through proclaiming the gospel to those deeply loved by Him, and without the hope of a Savior. Make no mistakes about it, fulfilling this calling is costly; it was costly for Jesus and it will be costly for us as well.

The first question in the *Heidelberg Catechism* is "What is your only comfort in life and in death?" The Catechism answers: "That I am not my own, but belong—body and soul, in life and in death—to my faithful Savior, Jesus Christ. He has fully paid for all my sins with his precious blood, and has set me free from the tyranny of the devil. He also watches over me in such a way that not a hair can fall from my head without the will of my Father in heaven; in fact, all things must work together for my salvation. Because I belong to him, Christ, by his Holy Spirit, assures me of eternal life and makes me wholeheartedly willing and ready from now on to live for him." The Catechism's answer invites us to consider the price of our calling and the rewards that are offered to those who are faithful. Because our debt of sin has been paid in full and we are secure in our salvation, we can become "wholeheartedly willing and ready from now on to live for him."

Dying for the gospel is much easier than living for it. Although momentarily painful, the experience of death will quickly pass, and we are ushered into heaven. It's much harder to deny yourself and surrender day by day to the will of God. Are you wholeheartedly willing to live for His glory? The message of Jesus' words and example is clear: God's glory is worth it.

Made in the USA
Coppell, TX
22 December 2022